TALES FROM THE LOCKER ROOM

TALES FROM THE LOCKER ROOM

Sports Scandals And Controversies

Angus G. Garber III

SMITHMARK

A FRIEDMAN GROUP BOOK

This edition published in 1992
by SMITHMARK Publishers Inc.
112 Madison Avenue
New York, New York 10016

ISBN 0-8317-7985-3

TALES FROM THE LOCKER ROOM
Sports Scandals and Controversies
was prepared and produced by
Michael Friedman Publishing Group, Inc.
15 West 26th Street
New York, NY 10010

Editor: Sharon Kalman
Art Director: Jeff Batzli
Designer: Kevin Ullrich
Photography Researcher: Daniella Jo Nilva

Typeset by The Typecrafters Inc.
Color separation by Scantrans Pte. Ltd.
Printed and bound in Hong Kong by Leefung-Asco Printers Ltd.

SMITHMARK Books are available for bulk purchase for sales promotions and premium use.
For details write or telephone the Manager of Special Sales, SMITHMARK Publishers Inc.,
112 Madison Avenue, New York, New York 10016. (212) 532-6600.

DEDICATION

For Lynde Eliot May III and Angus Gregory Garber I, two larger-than-life influences.

CONTENTS

After a seven-year retirement, Jim Palmer attempted to become the first Hall of Famer to return to the major league. But he didn't make it much further than spring training.

INTRODUCTION

There was a time, a kinder, gentler era if you will, when sports arenas were the few places where Everyfan could consistently escape from reality. Certainly scandal, corruption, and controversy have always lurked just beneath the surface of athletics, but around the turn of the century, people weren't always looking for the frayed edges of human weakness.

All of that changed in 1919, when the Chicago White Sox fixed the World Series and deliberately lost to the Cincinnati Reds. "Shoeless" Joe Jackson, one of history's finest hitters, was barred from baseball for life, along with seven other players. The Black Sox scandal is the modern line of demarcation, the precise moment in time where innocence was lost and disillusionment was found; the field of dreams gone sour. That the decadent 1920s, as chronicled by F. Scott Fitzgerald, were to follow was hardly a coincidence. "They were careless people, Tom and Daisy," Fitzgerald wrote in *The Great Gatsby*, published in 1925. "They smashed up things and creatures and then retreated back into their money or their vast carelessness, or whatever it was that kept them together, and let other people clean up the mess they had made."

And what a mess the world of sports has become. As the years have passed, unbridled joy has hardened into brittle cynicism. There is still great beauty to be found in a breathtaking Eric Dickerson touchdown run, a searing Wade Boggs double off the Green Monster at Fenway Park, or an elegant twelve-meter yacht, spinnaker billowing under full sail. But the headlines of retirement, extortion, extramarital affairs, and ludicrous *pro forma* court battles are often not far behind. Lately, reality seems to have intruded on sports to the point of suffocation. It is indeed a vicious cycle. High schools are charged with illegally recruiting top athletes; college programs are put on probation or even abolished for ignoring the basic code of morals, not to mention education; professional teams look the other way as their stars struggle with substance abuse or other addictive behaviors. The agony transcends mere defeat, running far ahead of the ecstacy.

Check your rose-colored glasses at the door.

The sight of running back Eric Dickerson bolting through a tiny crack at the line of scrimmage and breaking free is almost poetic. Off the field, however, Dickerson has a reputation as a whining self-centered athlete and a history of squabbles with management.

Less than five years after he broke one of baseball's most cherished records, Pete Rose was doing time for allegedly gambling on his Cincinnati Reds.

© Edward L. Taylor/FPG International

Even Pete Rose, the most prolific hitter in baseball history, succumbed in the end. Less than five years after he surpassed Ty Cobb's record of 4,191 hits, Rose, the Cincinnati Reds manager at the time, was banned from baseball for life for allegedly gambling on his own team. He can't even buy a ticket to a ball game. And yet Rose's affliction is nothing new. In 1963, National Football League Commissioner Pete Rozelle banished for life Green Bay's Paul Hornung and Alex Karras of Detroit for gambling on their own games. In 1983, Rozelle ruled similarly against Indianapolis quarterback Art Schlichter. Denny McLain, a member of the Detroit Tigers and the last pitcher to win thirty games in one season, went to jail on a variety of charges two years later. In a ridiculous posture, Baseball Commissioner Bowie Kuhn forced Willie Mays and Mickey Mantle to sever their ties with baseball after they took jobs with Atlantic City casinos long after their playing days were over. Eventually, they were both reinstated by Kuhn's successor, Peter Ueberroth.

Others weren't so lucky. The Israeli athletes murdered by terrorists at the 1972 Summer Olympic Games in Munich, West Germany, had no second chance. The same is true of South Korean boxer Duk Koo Kim, who died at the hands of Ray "Boom Boom" Mancini in 1982. In 1985, thirty-nine soccer spectators died when hooliganism raged out of control at the European Cup final. The same year, Philadelphia Flyers goalie Pelle Lindbergh died at the wheel of his Porsche 930 Turbo. Police say he was driving approximately eighty miles an hour under the influence of alcohol. Maryland basketball player Len Bias and Cleveland Browns defensive back Don Rogers, linked forever by a weakness for cocaine, died of drug overdoses within three days of each other in the spring of 1986. There are still questions about the heart-breaking, on-court 1990 death of Loyola-Marymount basketball star Hank Gathers. The link between inner-city murders and those who covet flashy, expensive sneakers is equally disturbing.

© Tim DeFrisco/Allsport

Hank Gathers was a gifted college basketball player who never had the chance to reach the professional arena.

© Mike Valeri/FPG International

Every sports franchise has its skeletons in the closet. The Indianapolis Colts left Baltimore under the cover of darkness in 1984; six years later the New England Patriots won one of sixteen games, and owner Victor Kiam managed to offend an entire nation in the wake of the Lisa Olson locker-room affair.

Hitters claimed that Houston Astros pitcher Mike Scott scuffed his baseballs to make his fastballs more effective, but no evidence was ever found.

© Robert Beck/Allsport

The basic business of sports has been revealed in repeated labor disputes and antitrust suits that seem only to hurt the fans. When Al Davis moved the Oakland Raiders to the Los Angeles Coliseum, he was simply following tradition. In 1957, the Brooklyn Dodgers and New York Giants pulled up stakes to relocate to Los Angeles and San Francisco respectively. In 1984, Baltimore Colts owner Robert Irsay packed up the moving vans at midnight and stole away for Indianapolis. Four years later, gold-digging Cardinals owner William Bidwill moved his NFL franchise to Phoenix and gouged the local customers with the NFL's steepest ticket price. In this age of free agency, even our heroes rarely sit still for very long. Did New York Yankees owner George Steinbrenner really fire manager Billy Martin five different times? Basketball coach Larry Brown moves more times than Mayflower Van Lines.

As technology improves, so do the methods of cheating. Bats are corked, balls are scuffed with subtle care. Certain nations have reportedly mastered the art of blood-doping, the practice of injecting athletes with their own stockpiled, oxygen-rich blood before competition. Steroids blazed across the world's consciousness when it was discovered that Canadian sprinter Ben Johnson's world-record speed was a result of bigger muscles through chemistry.

© Bob Thomas Sports Photography

For a fleeting moment, Canada's Ben Johnson was the world's fastest man. And then he was revealed to be a fraud when traces of steroids were found in his blood at the 1988 Summer Olympics.

Occasionally, beyond the heavy-handed tabloid headlines, there is whimsical controversy to remind us of the true function of sports: entertainment and escape. There is *Sports Illustrated* debuting its shocking swimsuit issue in 1964; Darryl "Chocolate Thunder" Dawkins delightedly slam-dunking two backboards and sending shards of glass flying everywhere; and George Brett and the infamous "Pine Tar Incident." There is also Anne White, Jan Stephenson, and Molly "Machine Gun" Bolin showing us that sports clearly has a softer side.

Here it is, the wide range of insidious scandal and frivolous controversy in twentieth-century sports. Check your rose-colored glasses at the door.

© UPI/Bettmann Newsphotos

The 1919 Chicago White Sox looked for all the world like a typical gritty ballclub in their team photograph. After they lost the World Series, however, the "Pale Hose" and their leader Joe Jackson were exposed as a team of cheats.

BLACK SOX THROW SERIES

Chicago's American League entry began the 1919 season as the White Sox. They went 88-52 over the regular season, 3½ games ahead of the Cleveland Indians, to win the pennant. Left-fielder Joe Jackson hit .351 and drove in ninety-six runs to send the ChiSox into the World Series against the Cincinnati Reds. However, after losing the series to the Reds, four games to three, it was discovered that several members of the team had taken money from gamblers to intentionally lose. In turn, that Chicago team became known as the Black Sox.

Exactly what happened will never be known. Pitcher Eddie Cicotte, the ace of the staff, opened the Series and allowed five Cincinnati runs in the fourth inning. The Reds won 9-1 and rumors were flying in the gambling underworld. In the end, Chicago won three games but succumbed in the eighth game, 10-5. The Reds scored four first-inning runs off of starter Lefty Williams, who lost his third game of the Series.

A year later, an investigation led to a public trial which fell short of explaining the specifics of the case. Before the official proceedings, player depositions, some of them damning, disappeared without a trace. Eventually, all of the White Sox were acquitted. Still, Williams, Cicotte, Jackson, and five other Chicago teammates were all banned by Baseball Commissioner Kenesaw Mountain Landis for their part in the alleged fix.

Jackson, who hit twelve times in thirty-two at-bats for a splendid .375 average, always maintained his innocence in the affair. Research done in recent years seems to indicate that he was telling the truth. The famous line attributed to a young boy waiting outside the grand jury chamber, "Say it ain't so, Joe," was probably created by a New York newspaper columnist with an overactive imagination.

There was nothing imagined, however, about the pall cast over baseball when the news surfaced. The age of innocence was over and sports were never quite the same.

TUNNEY SURVIVES LONG COUNT

Even without the fuel of controversy, it was one of the greatest sports spectacles ever. In one corner was the champion, wearing white trunks, Gene Tunney. In the opposite corner, wearing dark trunks, was Jack Dempsey. A total of 104,943 spectators paid $2,658,660 at Chicago's Soldier Field to see the two heavyweight boxers square off in a ballyhooed rematch on September 10, 1927.

Tunney had taken Dempsey's world heavyweight title a year earlier in a decision in Philadelphia, but Dempsey said he was ready for revenge. Tunney had the best of it in the early rounds, but a Dempsey left hook in the seventh round caught him on the side of the chin. A second left hook staggered Tunney and Dempsey swarmed in. He issued a right, a left, and another right. Tunney went down. Dempsey, thinking the fight was over, went to the nearest corner and rested on the ropes.

While Tunney raised himself to a sitting position, referee Dave Barry ordered Dempsey to the opposite, neutral corner. When

Dempsey refused, Barry strode across the ring and pushed him toward the far corner. Then, at least four seconds after Tunney had gone down, Barry began the mandatory ten-count. At the count of nine Tunney began to rise to his feet and at ten his clear eyes convinced Barry he could continue.

Dempsey was on top of Tunney again in a second, pressing and flinging leather, but Tunney regained his senses. Tunney surprised Dempsey with a straight right hand to the head and one to the chin. Dempsey's legs buckled momentarily and his heart flagged—he had lost his will. His opportunity was gone. Tunney would win another ten-round decision, but to this day fight fans debate whether Tunney would have risen in time for a legitimate ten-count.

Jack Dempsey's stubborn nature might have cost him this famed 1927 fight with Gene Tunney. Here, referee Dave Barry tries to push Dempsey into a neutral corner while Tunney collects his thoughts.

'FIGHTING FINISH' AT DERBY

Back in the days before instant replay, sports were largely unregulated, and no one could hold up an incriminating videotape cassette after it was all over.

© UPI/Bettmann Newsphotos

Jockeys Herb Fisher (number 9) and Don Meade tangle down the stretch of the 1933 Kentucky Derby.

In the 1933 Kentucky Derby, two jockeys battled it out down the stretch. Herb Fisher, riding Head Play, was leading the Derby as the horses headed down the upper stretch. When he spotted Broker's Tip and jockey Don Meade trying to slide by on the inside rail, Fisher swiftly guided Head Play toward the inside.

Meade reached out his right hand to prevent Fisher from "putting me through the fence. I pushed him off me to get running room." Fisher responded by grabbing Meade. They rode that way together down the stretch. As they approached the finish, Fisher hit Meade in the head several times with his whip. Meade hit back.

It was a close finish. The placing judges put their heads together and declared Broker's Tip the winner.

A CLOSE SHAVE FOR COLLEGE BASKETBALL

College athletes, struggling along without any visible means of income, have always been a vulnerable target. Gamblers, in particular, have historically taken advantage of the athletes' situations. College basketball, a rising comet in the late 1940s and early 1950s, attracted high-rollers for the first time. In January 1951, Junius Kellogg of Manhattan College informed the Bronx District

In 1951, Junius Kellogg refused to fix games involving the Manhattan College basketball team. His sense of ethics resulted in a handful of indictments and suggested that college basketball was not the pure sport the public believed.

Attorney that he had been approached and offered a bribe to shave points. He said he refused.

Point-shaving is difficult to detect because it doesn't involve losing outright. Players accept money from gamblers, who size up the point-spread and bet against the team they are bribing. Thus, if a bought player misses a few shots or makes a critical turnover here or there he can influence the score. Since most point-spreads are ten points or less, a few mistakes can easily alter the result for bettors.

An investigation in 1951 revealed that several of Kellogg's Manhattan teammates had accepted bribes, and, ultimately, players from Manhattan College, City College, Long Island University, and New York University were indicted.

During the 1978-79 season, a government informer said he paid off three Boston College basketball players to shave points. Rick Kuhn, Jim Sweeny, and later Ernie Cobb accepted $2,500 per game, according to the gambler. He said he won on six of the nine fixed Boston College games and made nearly $100,000.

In 1990, the specter of point-shaving returned to college basketball. An anonymous former player at North Carolina State University admitted he had accepted gambling money in exchange for point-shaving. The case was probed by the North Carolina State Bureau of Investigation, though the allegations were never substantiated in court.

Ouch!

In 1950, boxer Vic Towell knocked down opponent Danny Sullivan fourteen times in a single bout. Needless to say, it was a victory for Towell, and a modern record.

HOGAN'S ONE-IRON PINCHED

Ben Hogan survived a bloody automobile crash in 1949, and performed marvelously in his debut eleven months later at the Los Angeles Open. By early summer of 1950, Hogan had completely regained his form. However, in the process of winning the 1950 United States Open at Merion, he had the unfortunate experience of losing his prized one-iron.

It was probably lifted by a fan, or perhaps an enemy. In any case, Hogan went most of his life without the club that served him so well. Rumors of its location have fascinated collectors for years, but recently a national collector purchased what he believed to be the club and had it shipped (thirty-three years after the theft) to the reticent Hogan at his home in Texas.

Hogan, overjoyed, confirmed that the club with the dime-sized worn spot in the middle of the blade was his long-lost one-iron. It is now on display at the United States Golf Association Golf House in Far Hills, New Jersey.

Boxing toll mounts in 1953

In 1953, boxing suffered the deaths of twenty-two fighters in the ring. It was the worst year ever for fatalities involving the sweet science.

LEWIS CRIMSON AFTER TACKLE

Rice University halfback Dickie Moegle thought he was in the clear. In the second quarter of the 1954 Cotton Bowl, he had sprinted just past the line of scrimmage, and all the way to the end zone. That's because all the University of Alabama defenders were somewhere in his wake as he ran down the sideline. What Moegle didn't count on was the sudden presence of a twelfth man.

Rice already led, 7-6, and the thought of another enemy score worked on the mind of Crimson Tide fullback Tommy Lewis. He sprang off the bench and dragged down a startled Moegle. Officials, realizing that Lewis was on the field illegally, credited Moegle with a ninety-five-yard touchdown run. Rice eventually won, 28-6, but Lewis' impromptu tackle is the play that people remember.

Say It Ain't So, Joe

Joltin' Joe DiMaggio, the Yankee Clipper, married Marilyn Monroe in January 1954. But the romance was short-lived: Nine months later, the dapper former ballplayer and the voluptuous Hollywood starlet divorced.

CRASH KILLS VUCKOVICH

No automobile race captures the imagination of America like the Indianapolis 500. With more than 100,000 fans in the stands at the Indianapolis Speedway in 1955, Bill Vuckovich lost control of his Hopkins Special and crashed. He died from the injuries he sustained, but his sons carried his name with honor in later years at the Old Brickyard.

© Wide World Photos

In 1955, auto racer Bill Vuckovich crashed and died at the Indianapolis Speedway. Ironically, his grandson would later be claimed in an accident behind the wheel.

The eyes have it

The sight of umpires has been questioned by players and fans since baseball began in the nineteenth century. In 1955, Eddie Rommel confirmed what many of them had believed all along! He became the first major league umpire to wear glasses on the field.

GIANTS, DODGERS GO WEST

To many devoted fans, a sports franchise is a sacred thing. It is something in which we put our trust, our faith, and whatever residual enthusiasm we have after a hard week at the office. In 1957, the New York Giants and Brooklyn Dodgers broke thousands of hearts by pulling up stakes and bolting for the West Coast. It was the biggest jump a professional baseball franchise had ever taken, over three thousand miles.

According to Giants president Horace C. Stoneham, it was a move based not on emotion but reality. "We had to go now, because if we delayed, such a favorable opportunity might not present itself again," Stoneham said. "I am as sentimental a New Yorker as anyone else, but we simply didn't draw here."

The Dodgers offered a similar explanation, and so Gil Hodges, Sandy Koufax, Duke Snider, and Don Zimmer all packed their

"We had to go now, because if we delayed, such a favorable opportunity might not present itself again. I am as sentimental a New Yorker as anyone else, but we simply didn't draw here."

21

Roy Campanella was a terror at the plate, with a bat and with a glove, too. An auto accident tragically shortened his Hall of Fame career.

bags and headed for Los Angeles. Similarly, Giants manager Bill Rigney brought Willie Mays and Hank Sauer with him to San Francisco. On this occasion, the Giants left their heart at the old Polo Grounds.

CAMPANELLA PARALYZED

He was a feared hitter and a superb defensive catcher for the Dodgers during their last ten seasons in Brooklyn. Tragically, Roy Campanella's career ended about the same time the Dodgers left town for Los Angeles.

A muscular five-foot-ten, 190 pounds, Campanella was paralyzed in a car accident while driving home in the snow. He never ran the base paths again.

In 1969, the Baseball Hall of Fame recognized his greatness. The man who stroked 242 home runs and drove in 856 runs in ten seasons was enshrined at Cooperstown, New York.

IT'S AMAZIN': METS LOSE 120

How bad can it get? In 1962 the fledgling New York Mets, managed by Casey Stengel, somehow lost 120 of 160 games. That's a winning percentage of .250 and a major-league record for all time.

The "Amazin'" Mets didn't have much hitting, pitching, or defense, but other than that they were terrific. Rightfielder Richie Ashburn hit .306 that inaugural season but, sadly, the feat didn't rub off on his teammates. Marv Throneberry hit .244, pitcher Roger Craig lost twenty-four of thirty-four decisions, and the Mets finished 60½ games behind the San Francisco Giants.

No matter. After the Mets' 51-111 season in 1963, they eventually righted themselves. With Tom Seaver pitching and Cleon Jones hitting, the 1969 Miracle Mets won the National League's East Division, winning 100 games. They went on to sweep the Atlanta Braves in the Championship Series, then hammered the Baltimore Orioles in four of five World Series games. Amazing.

NFL SACKS KARRAS, HORNUNG

He was the quintessential golden boy. Paul Hornung, blond and handsome, played college football at Notre Dame, home of the famed Golden Dome, and won the Heisman Trophy in 1956. An ethereal runner, Hornung was the first overall selection in the 1957 National Football League draft. He went to the Green Bay Packers and helped transform one of the league's weaker teams into a powerhouse.

Hornung won the NFL scoring title for three consecutive seasons, 1959 to 1961. His 176-point total in 1960 was a record. In 1963, however, the luster faded when young commissioner Pete Rozelle suspended Hornung and Detroit Lions defensive lineman Alex Karras for gambling on league games. The revelations sent shock waves through the NFL.

They were both reinstated a year later by Rozelle and Hornung continued to shine. Twenty years after his last game, the writers who covered the NFL finally voted to enshrine him at the Pro Football Hall of Fame in Canton, Ohio.

All that glitters is not gold, and so it was with Paul Hornung, the 1956 Heisman Trophy winner. Seven years later, the Green Bay Packers' running back was suspended, along with the Detroit Lions' Alex Karras, for gambling.

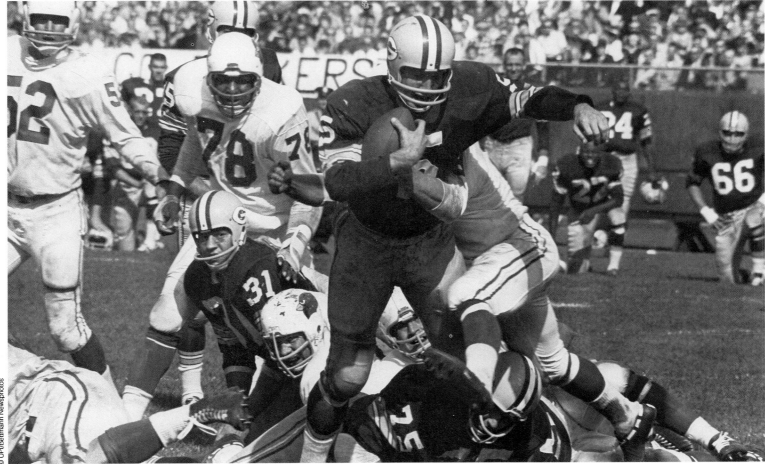

Sports Illustrated unveils swimsuit issue

These days, the annual swimsuit issue from *Sports Illustrated* generates the kind of anticipation usually reserved for the Super Bowl and the World Series. But back in 1964 it was the brainchild of the magazine's managing editor, Andre Laguerre, and Jule Campbell, a fashion reporter. Their idea was to bring a breath of summer into the lives of its readers early each February—or something to that effect.

Babette, a popular model in the 1960s, was featured in a five-page spread that was dwarfed by a thirteen-page travel section devoted to snorkeling in the Caribbean. As time passed, *Sports Illustrated* caught on and reversed the ratio of travel to swimsuits.

While critics point out that there is more than sports being illustrated in the ever-burgeoning photo layouts, there is a wholesome quality to the magazine's package. The *Sports Illustrated* swimsuit issue is one of modeling's hottest jobs, since it has helped promote the careers of Cheryl Tiegs, Christie Brinkley, and Paulina Porizkova.

Early on, though, the magazine learned that a coy approach seemed to pique subscriber interest. To that end, *Sports Illustrated*'s models have been breathlessly wholesome and reasonably well covered. The possible exception is the famous Walter Iooss Jr. photograph of Tiegs, just about all of her, in a white fishnet tank suit.

Since its inception, interest in the issue has steadily, and dramatically, increased. In 1988, the swimsuit issue sold 1.88 million newsstand copies, twelve times the usual amount.

SPROINNNG! ASTROTURF IS INVENTED

Prior to April 12, 1965, baseball and football were all-natural sports without any additives or preservatives. And then one fateful day, professional athletics were changed forever. AstroTurf reared its ugly, advanced-polymers head.

The Eighth Wonder of the World, the Houston Astrodome, was home to the Houston Astros. Winning the National League pennant at the time seemed easier than getting grass to grow indoors. And so, when the wondrous chemical engineers at Monsanto developed AstroTurf, the Astrodome was its logical first home. The ball seemed to skip off the phoney grass like a cueball on a pool table, and the players said it hurt their ankles to play on what was essentially an asphalt parking lot.

Today AstroTurf and other varieties of faux grass grace many of the world's finest sporting venues. The players still aren't thrilled to have to play on it, but it seems to have entrenched itself on the sporting landscape.

Back in 1967, before the women's movement gained momentum, Jock Semple gave it a big push. The Boston Marathon official tried to interfere with the ground-breaking run of Kathrine Switzer, but was rebuffed.

Boston run-in

Jock Semple, a Boston Marathon official, tried to interfere with Kathrine Switzer (entrant number 261), when she broke the male stranglehold on the event in 1967. Semple was unceremoniously knocked away by several male runners and women soon became a staple of the event.

SOCCER HOOLIGANS
BRING ON TRAGEDY

The striker deftly moves the ball around a defender, maneuvers into the clear, drills a missile past a sprawling goalie, and more than 40,000 fans stand as one. A crowd's collective ecstasy can be a beautiful thing to behold. The downside, of course, is a case of mass hysteria waiting to happen if things don't go well for the home side. Over the years, soccer has been dogged by flashes of hooliganism that have wrought tragedy.

The watershed event occurred on May 25, 1964, at National Stadium in Lima, Peru. The home team, Peru's National Squad, was in the process of being hopelessly outplayed by Argentina in a pre-Olympic soccer playoff when the restless, frustrated crowd found a rallying point. Peru, trailing 6-1, seemed to salvage a little pride with a goal in the final moments, but referee R. Angel Pazos nullified the score and signaled for a rough-play foul. Incensed, two Peruvian fans charged the field. And then all hell broke loose.

As the crowd roared, Pazos quickly stopped the game. Many of the 50,000 spectators ran for the exits and some, amid fires blazing in the stands, were pinned against locked iron gates. In all, 318 people died of trampling or asphyxiation; more than five hundred others were injured.

It was a scene that has repeated itself, though not on such a numbing scale. On May 29, 1985, Liverpool from England and Juventus from Turin, Italy, met in the European Cup soccer final in Brussels' Heysel Stadium. During the match, English hooligans, many of them incoherent after a day of drinking, charged a group of Italian fans, who ran from them in terror. Thirty-nine spectators, thirty-one of them Italian, were crushed at the bottom of Section 2. Incredibly, the game was allowed to continue and Juventus earned a hollow victory.

Following the tragedy, the Union of European Football Associations voted to bar British teams from competing in Europe. Four years later, only a week after the UEFA considered lifting the ban, with the exception of the Liverpool team, disaster struck again.

At the National Cup semifinal match at Sheffield's Hillsborough Stadium, Liverpool fans were involved in a gruesome incident with their Nottingham Forest rivals. Ninety-four Liverpool fans died, many of them crushed against a steel fence that had been erected to contain hooligans. Police inadvertently caused the massacre by allowing some three thousand angry fans milling outside the stadium to enter the Leppings Lane gate when it appeared those in front might be crushed. That wave of humanity ran down a tunnel, then pressed the victims, many of them legitimate ticket holders, against the fence.

Experts say Britain is prone to hooliganism because of the short distance between rival cities and rampant unemployment. Bitterness, boredom, and the prospect of a bleak future move the worst of the hooligans to make trouble, which Britain's outmoded stadiums are ill-equipped to handle.

Though violence in American stadiums hasn't yet come to this frightening stage, the potential is always there. Alcohol, available in most stadiums, stokes the fire, and occasional drunken fistfights

The angry crowd at Brussels' Heysel Stadium, fueled by alcohol, swarmed out of control at the 1985 European Cup soccer final between Liverpool and Juventus.

are now part of today's sporting landscape. The lesson of soccer hooliganism suggests that the time when the action spills from the field and into the stands is never far away.

ALI BANNED FROM BOXING

As the heavyweight champion of the world, Muhammad Ali made a living fighting with his fists. But when he was called to fight in Vietnam, he drew the line. In 1967, he refused his local draft board on the basis of his Muslim faith.

Even when it would have been more expedient and more popular for the champion to serve his limited time and get back to

Muhammad Ali roared when he knocked out Sonny Liston, but his passion and beliefs were severely tested when he was jailed for failing to fight in the Vietnam War.

the business of boxing, he was a powerfully conscientious objector to America's war in Asia, saying: "I ain't got no quarrel with them Viet Cong." He was banished from boxing for three years, which is like an eternity in the brief life of a world-class athlete.

And yet, when he returned, he was still the most popular and visible athlete, and perhaps man, in the world. Ali regained his championship and he never lost his dignity.

Slam dunked!

With Lew Alcindor (later known as Kareem Abdul-Jabbar) of UCLA and the University of Houston's Elvin Hayes dominating college basketball high above the rim, the sport's braintrust moved to ban the dunk in 1967. In retrospect, it was about as wise and successful as Prohibition.

Nine years later, the dunk was declared a legal shot again.

SCHRANZ MISSES GATE; KILLY WINS THIRD GOLD

Jean-Claude Killy, idol of the French nation, had already won two gold medals at the 1968 Winter Olympic Games in Grenoble, France. He had won a close race in the all-or-nothing downhill, and coasted to an easier victory in the giant slalom. And now, he prepared for the slalom and a chance to equal Austrian Toni Sailor's sweep in the 1956 Games at Cortina, Italy.

Sure enough, Killy led after the first run. Still, many skiers were within striking distance, one of them Austria's Karl Schranz. In a race that featured fog and soft, wet snow, Killy weaved judiciously through the poles on the course. Schranz, charging down the hill, beat Killy's time by a half-second. But there was a problem. Officials claimed that Schranz missed a gate. Television replays, limited by the oppressive fog, were inconclusive. Still, Schranz was disqualified and Killy was awarded his third gold medal.

HEIDI BOOTS JETS-RAIDERS

The New York Jets, carried by quarterback Joe Namath, led the Oakland Raiders 32-29 with sixy-five seconds left in the 1968 game. Since it was coming up on 7 P.M. in the East, the National Broadcasting Corporation faced a tough decision: stay with the game or switch over to *Heidi*, a special movie for children.

The Jets and the Raiders faded to black and suddenly, the hills were alive with the sound of, well, Heidi. Imagine the viewers' surprise when they read their newspapers the next morning. Impossibly, the Raiders scored two late touchdowns and won, 43-32. NBC had authored one of the great debacles in the history of televised sport.

MAKI DECKS GREEN

Hockey is the fastest sport played by men under their own power. It is also, quite often, one of the most vulgar and wicked sports. Some people believe that fighting in the National Hockey League has reached epidemic levels. It has been around for as long as men have wielded sharp, curved sticks. One of the watershed events in hockey history was the battle between Ted Green and Wayne Maki.

September 21, 1969, was just another ordinary exhibition game between the Boston Bruins and St. Louis Blues in Ottawa, Canada. The Big Bad Bruins, as they were known in those days, were a team short on finesse and long on clout in the corners. One of their leading terminators was Green. The Blues' Maki was not one to be intimidated, though. Their brief on-ice meeting caused national repercussions.

Maki hacked at Green after words had been exchanged. Green took a swipe at Maki, who went down hard. As Green turned and skated up ice, Maki pulled himself to his feet, caught Green from behind, raised his stick high over his head, and with both hands brought it crashing down on Green's unprotected head. Later, in the hospital, it was determined that Green had a fractured

© UPI/Bettmann Newsphotos

skull. The insertion of a metal plate and two involved operations eventually enabled Green to return to the ice.

Following the incident, the NHL suspended both players for thirty days and fined them $300. Referees were instructed to issue match penalties for stick-swinging incidents. Meanwhile, the Ottawa district attorney filed criminal charges against both Green and Maki, a NHL first. They were both charged with assault and the case went to court, where it was prominently played in the national media. Both players were acquitted, but the NHL had been stained deeply. Today, the fighting continues.

MCLAIN STRIKES OUT

There was no better pitcher in baseball than Denny McLain in the late 1960s. In 1968, he won thirty-one games and lost only six for the Detroit Tigers on his way to both the American League's Most Valuable Player Award and the Cy Young Award. In 1969 he was 24-9 and shared the Cy Young with Baltimore's Mike Cuellar. And that was pretty much that.

In 1970, McLain's penchant for trouble began to surface. He was suspended from baseball when it was alleged that he was involved in bookmaking three seasons earlier. He was reinstated later, but appeared in only fourteen games, winning three of eight decisions. The Tigers traded him to the Washington Senators, and only two seasons after he had led the American League in victories, he recorded more defeats, twenty-two, than any other pitcher. One year later, McLain was out of baseball entirely.

His struggle with the law, however, continued. In 1985, he was found guilty of a long list of charges such as racketeering, extortion, and possession of thirteen kilos of cocaine. He was sentenced to twenty-three years in prison. Nearly thirty months later, his conviction was overturned by a federal court of appeals and inmate number 04000-018 left the Federal Correctional Institution in Talladega, Florida. Baseball, he said, probably wasn't in his future.

The mouth that roared

On September 21, 1970, announcer Howard Cosell made his debut with ABC Television's Monday Night Football. Critics were quick to pan Cosell, but his condescending pomposity scored in the rating wars. "I don't care if they love me or hate me," Cosell said, "as long as they keep watching."

OPENING UP BASEBALL'S FREE AGENT FLOODGATE

There was a time when baseball players were mere mortals, when they made an honest wage for an honest effort. Then, midway through the 1990 season, the Oakland Athletics announced they would pay right fielder Jose Canseco $5 million a season to catch and hit a baseball. That's $30,864.20 per game. Canseco, like many major-league players today, may not even know who Curt Flood was, but he should. Flood is the reason some of today's marginal players are taking home close to $1 million a season.

"I don't care if they love me or hate me, as long as they keep watching."

Curt Flood had played twelve years for the St. Louis Cardinals when he turned thirty-two on January 18, 1970. He compiled a fine .293 career batting average and had been among the league's leaders in at-bats. In 1964, his 211 hits led the National League. Coming off a .285 season, in which he was paid $90,000, he was traded to the Philadelphia Phillies, who offered him $100,000.

The phone call was a shock. Flood burst into tears. "I'm not going to let them do this to me," he told friend Marian Jorgensen. "They say that if I don't go to Philadelphia, I don't play at all. Right there, they shoot down my rights. They shoot me down as a man. I won't stand for it."

"The lightning had struck. The dream lay shattered. It was a bad scene," he wrote in his autobiography, *The Way It Is*. "To challenge the sanctity of organized baseball was to question one of the primary myths of American culture. To persist in the heresy required profound conviction, with endurance to match."

And Flood had vast reserves of both. In a letter to Baseball Commissioner Bowie Kuhn, Flood challenged the sport's reserve clause, calling it illegal and immoral. He said he believed his tenure gave him the right to consider offers from other teams. Kuhn disagreed, saying he had signed a contract with St. Louis and the Cardinals had legally reassigned that contract to Philadelphia.

Flood hired former Supreme Court Justice Arthur J. Goldberg, one of the world's most visible lawyers, to press his case in the legal system. Goldberg advised Flood not to play during the 1970 season, so as not to jeopardize his case. On March 4, Judge Irving Ben Cooper denied Flood's requested injunction and recommended that the relative merits of the reserve system be dealt with in a trial. The baseball establishment claimed this would change "baseball as we know it." And they were right.

Baseball had been sued on similar grounds in the past but never by a player with Flood's marquee value, or a lawyer of Goldberg's stature. As the issue was debated across the nation as well as in Federal Court, Flood spent the 1970 season in voluntary exile in Denmark. It was a time of questioning authority that was crystallized on college campuses.

© Wide World Photos

A recent poll of today's major-league stars revealed that most had never heard of Curt Flood. Too bad. Flood's challenging of the free-agent system in 1970 opened the bank for modern players.

"I think Curt is doing a service to all players in the leagues, especially for the younger players coming up who are not superstars," said Jackie Robinson, the man who broke baseball's color line in 1947. "All he is asking for is the right to negotiate."

Flood lost the battle in court but won the war. His basic objection to a trade eventually forced major-league owners to create a viable free agency system, which allowed players to essentially listen to all offers. That led to wild spending and a handful of overnight millionaires. Flood signed with Washington Senators owner Bob Short in 1971, but played in only thirteen games before retiring. Still, his legacy lives on. Jose Canseco, take note.

DiVicenzo bogeys 19th

Roberto DiVicenzo had won the 1970 Masters, one of golfing's most cherished events, but he inadvertently signed the wrong card in the scorer's tent. "Oh, what a stupid I am," he said. With DiVicenzo disqualified, Billy Casper beat Gene Littler in a playoff.

Perry spits in authority's eye

Gaylord Perry was the National League's dominant pitcher in 1970. He won twenty-three games for the San Francisco Giants and lost only thirteen. And he did it with saliva.

Perry simply reinvented the spitter that had flourished in baseball's early days before it was banished. Perry carried the art of deceit to a higher level with a series of covert actions, such as sneaking spit on the ball, that foiled umpires at every turn.

Shepard's moon shot

In 1971, astronaut Alan Shepard hit one of the most famous golf shots ever. Undaunted by one of the largest hazards ever confronted, Shepard stepped onto the moon's surface and stroked an ironshot with the television camera rolling. It may still be in orbit.

Splat! That sound you just heard was Gaylord Perry's spitball exploding in the catcher's mitt. Though cheating had gone on in baseball for years, Perry, according to some of his peers, raised it to an art form.

© Wide World Photos

USSR stuns USA!

Before the 1972 Summer Olympic Games in Munich, West Germany, there were three things you could always count on: death, taxes, and a United States gold medal in men's basketball.

The nation that created basketball had gripped it so tightly since the sport was introduced in Olympic competition in 1936 that no other country had ever won the gold. At Munich, the United States progressed through the field as expected and, upon reaching the final against the USSR, had a string of sixty-two consecutive victories dating back to 1936.

And then the impossible happened on September 9. The USSR hung in the entire game, but it appeared the United States would win when the clock ran out. An official, however, awarded the ball to the USSR and insisted that time be put back on the clock. Final score: USSR 51, USA 50.

TRAGEDY STRIKES OLYMPIANS IN MUNICH

It was just before dawn on September 5, 1972, 4:30 A.M. to be precise, when the darkest cloud in the history of the Olympic Games descended directly on the drab building known as 31 Connollystrasse.

Eight members of the Palestinian Black September group, a terrorist organization, forced their way into the rooms where members of the Israeli delegation slept at the Summer Olympic Games in Munich, West Germany. The original plan was to capture the twenty-one athletes and administrators, but when the alarm was sounded, one Israeli was shot dead. Still, his brave action allowed nine comrades to escape. A horrific twenty-hour drama followed. Like a devastating automobile accident, it was painful to watch but impossible to avert one's eyes.

The sight of a hooded man on the balcony of 31 Connollystrasse haunted millions around the world who had tuned in to watch athletes from different nations competing in mere games. Late that afternoon, the Olympic Organizing Committee issued a

© Tony Duffy/Allsport

After sixty-two consecutive victories, the United States Olympic basketball team finally lost. Aided by a sympathetic official's ruling, the USSR team prevailed in the gold-medal game of 1972.

"I am sure that the public will agree that we cannot allow a handful of terrorists to destroy this nucleus of international cooperation and goodwill we have in the Olympic movement."

press release that stated, "The Olympic peace has been broken by an act of assassination by criminal terrorists. The whole civilized world condemns this barbaric crime, this horror. With deep respect for the victims and as a sign of sympathy with the hostages not yet released, this afternoon's sports events are being canceled."

Behind the scenes, a crisis committee was set up, but chaos reigned. The International Olympic Committee said publicly that kidnapping across national boundaries would not be tolerated, but in the end German officials bowed to the pressure and conceived a plan than was doomed to fail.

At a late-night meeting of the IOC's executive board, it was decided that the Games would proceed after a memorial mass the following morning, regardless of the outcome. Just before midnight, the council's seventy-one members were told that all the terrorists had been killed or captured and the remaining eleven hostages were safe. It wasn't until the early-morning hours that the sobering news was delivered. Jim McKay, ABC's anchorman at Munich, looked wearily into the camera and, his voice breaking, announced, "That's it. They're all gone."

The hostages and terrorists had been helicoptered to a military airfield where they were told they might escape. The hairtrigger terrorists, fearing they had been duped, began firing and threw hand grenades which flashed against the night sky. When it was over, all the Israelis, one policeman, and all but three of the terrorists were dead.

Beethoven's Funeral March was the theme at Olympic Stadium the next morning, as athletes and spectators from around the world mourned the loss. Beyond the grief was a global movement to halt the Games. Avery Brundage, in his final tour as IOC president, begged to differ. "We have only the strength of a great ideal," he said at the ceremony. "I am sure that the public will agree that we cannot allow a handful of terrorists to destroy this nucleus of international cooperation and goodwill we have in the Olympic movement."

The Games went on for the final scheduled day, but the movement was never quite the same. The daring antics of young

Soviet gymnast Olga Korbut and the brilliance of Finnish distance runner Lasse Viren passed almost unnoticed. The inevitable politicization of a pure, international sporting spectacle had come to pass. Four years earlier, in the previous Olympics in Mexico City, the seeds had been sown. South Africa, because of its policies of apartheid, was banned from participating. There were violent student demonstrations in which more than 250 were killed, and three medal ceremonies were marred by American demonstrations for black solidarity. There would be boycotts in 1980 and 1984, when the Soviet Union and the United States respectively hosted the Summer Olympics.

In Munich, the three surviving Palestinians were captured and jailed. Less than two months later they were free. German authorities released them after a threat from a Palestinian commando who had hijacked a Lufthansa plane.

WASHINGTON KNOCKS OUT TOMJANOVICH

No, this is not another boxing story. Believe it or not, this is a tale told on a basketball court, on December 9, 1972. It wasn't a fight, really. More like a one-punch knockout of an innocent man.

Kermit Washington, a six-foot-eight, 250-pound forward for the Los Angeles Lakers, was wrestling with the Houston Rockets' Kevin Kunnert when the Lakers' Kareem Abdul-Jabbar stepped in and pinned Washington's left arm. Nevertheless, Washington managed to deck Kunnert with his free arm. "Rocket" Rudy Tomjanovich, in an attempt to join Abdul-Jabbar as a peacemaker, entered the fray and received an explosive punch to the face from Washington. He lay in a heap for several minutes.

It wasn't until later that the severe damage was assessed. Tomjanovich suffered fractures of the nose, jaw, and skull, which was crushed inward a full inch. "I hit him instinctively," Washington said. "I had no idea who it was. It was an honest, unfortunate mistake."

Kermit Washington's powerful punch changed the landscape of the National Basketball Association, not to mention the face of Rudy Tomjanovich.

It was unfortunate for Tomjanovich, who was never quite the same, on the court or off. While Washington was suspended for sixty days and fined $10,000, Tomjanovich needed many operations to rebuild his face. He returned to basketball six years later, wearing a mask favored by hockey goalies. In 1979, a jury awarded Tomjanovich $3.1 million in an unprecedented case in sports.

© Wide World Photos

No one inside tennis was particularly surprised when, in 1973, Billie Jean King swept fifty-five-year-old Bobby Riggs in three sets in the "Battle of the Sexes." Still, it was regarded as a healthy blow against chauvinism.

KING CROWNS RIGGS

By 1973, the Women's Movement had already begun. And just when inertia had begun to set in, there was a hustling tennis huckster named Bobby Riggs to give it a new momentum.

Riggs, fifty-five years old, challenged Billie Jean King, then the best woman player in professional tennis. This followed King's successful match with Margaret Court, another top-ranked player, who was beaten by Riggs. It was called "The Battle of the Sexes."

"I can't just play for money," King said. "I have to play for a cause, and I think women were put down after Margaret played him."

The best-of-five-set match on September 20, 1973, would be played in the Houston Astrodome, televised nationally by ABC, and the winner would take home $100,000.

Riggs and King battled to a draw in the pre-match hype department.

"She will crack up during the match," Riggs said.

"He's just an old man," King responded.

As it turned out, King was a little closer to the truth. Though Riggs was rated a 5-2 favorite, King's powerful groundstrokes and volleys were too much for him. Before a crowd in excess of thirty thousand, King beat Riggs in straight sets, 6-4, 6-3, 6-4.

CLEMENTE DIES IN AIR CRASH

Roberto Clemente's historical place on the baseball field was already clearly established in 1973, but somehow it wasn't enough. In eighteen years as the Pittsburgh Pirates' extraordinary out-fielder, Clemente had batted for a sparkling .317 average and produced exactly three thousand hits, 240 of them home runs. He was a hero to the nation from which he came, Puerto Rico. Clemente could have celebrated New Year's Eve, 1973, along with the rest of his countrymen, but he had a loftier ambition.

He had chartered a plane, loaded it with supplies, and was planning on flying to Nicaragua, where an earthquake had laid Managua bare. The plane, several tons overweight, developed engine trouble shortly after takeoff, and the pilot attempted to return to San Juan. One mile offshore, the plane crashed and the flame of Roberto Walker Clemente was snuffed. His body was never recovered.

Baseball took care of its own. Seven months after his death, the Hall of Fame waived its five-year eligibility rule and Clemente was enshrined at Cooperstown, New York.

Love match

They were America's cutest couple in 1974. Jimmy Connors and Chris Evert won each other's hearts and then each won tennis' grand event, Wimbledon. Clearly, this was a love-love match. They were engaged to be married, but it didn't quite work out. Connors wound up with a Playboy centerfold and Evert married England's John Lloyd. She has since divorced him and married former Olympic skier Andy Mills.

Namath takes hosing

He had been sacked by hulking defensive ends, intercepted by muscular cornerbacks, but never had he, uh, run into this kind of trouble.

On national television, Joe Namath modeled a popular brand of panty hose and seemed to enjoy it. The New York Jets' quarterback took home a tidy paycheck for the experience. He also intercepted a few passes off the field after displaying his famous legs.

THIS BUD'S FOR CLEVELAND

The relationship between alcohol and professional sports has always been an uneasy one. Some fans are rabid enough, even before the courage supplied by beer. Most ballparks shut off the taps late in the game, but in 1974 the Cleveland Indians stoked the potential fire with "Nickel Beer Night."

The Texas Rangers were the opponent, but by the middle innings fights were erupting all over Municipal Stadium among the fans. Before the game was over, Texas outfielder Jeff Burroughs had to be rescued from an ugly mob.

PREFONTAINE'S LUCK RUNS OUT

He was America's best and brightest long-distance runner. Steve Prefontaine was daring on the track and off it, as well. He had just run the second-fastest 5,000-meter race in United States history on May 30, 1975, when he stepped over the line for the last time. He flipped his convertible on a street in his hometown of Eugene, Oregon, and was crushed on impact. Lab results showed he was intoxicated, far over the legal limit.

Prefontaine, a four-time National Collegiate Athletic Association champion, had finished fourth in the 5,000-meter race at the 1972 Summer Olympics in Munich, West Germany. He turned down several lucrative offers to turn professional so that he might win the gold medal at Montreal in 1976. In the end, his style of hubris and bravado overshadowed his considerable substance.

© Wide World Photos

Like so many gifted athletes before him (and after), long-distance runner Steve Prefontaine couldn't come to grips with his ability. He died in 1975 in an alcohol-related automobile accident.

Deadly kiss of the spiderwoman

Two lovebirds in Aspen, Colorado, Spider Sabich and Claudine Longet were one of sports' glamour couples in 1976. Sabich, a former world professional skiing champion, and Longet, the former Mrs. Andy Williams, had lived together for nearly two years when their relationship came to a bloody end.

According to police reports, Sabich was demonstrating the use of a .22 caliber pistol for Longet at their home on March 21. Thinking the safety was on, Sabich handed the gun to Longet, who pulled the trigger twice, and said, "Bang. Bang." Sabich, thirty-three, died from stomach wounds inflicted by the shots.

Longet claimed it was an accident; prosecutors tried to suggest that there had been a separation in the offing. In any case, Longet was found guilty of criminally negligent homicide. She was fined $5,000 and served thirty days in jail with a two-year probation period.

Hayes intercepts Bauman

Ohio State football coach Woody Hayes, an institution in the Buckeye State, had a history of combative behavior. Over the years he had left a trail of bruised cameramen and fans who got a little

The same fire that drove coach Woody Hayes and his Ohio State University football teams to such glory undid him in the end. In the 1978 Gator Bowl, Hayes attacked an opposing player who intercepted an Ohio State pass and then went after one of his own players.

too close. In a sense, Clemson player Charlie Bauman got too close
for comfort in the 1978 Gator Bowl.

Clemson was hanging on to a tenuous 17-15 lead in Jackson-
ville, Florida, when Bauman stepped in front of an Art Schlichter
pass, intercepted it, and ran it out of bounds. As it happened, his
momentum took him into the path of the enraged Ohio State
coach. Bauman made the mistake of holding the ball aloft and
taunting Hayes, which sent him right over the edge. Shrewdly
picking the only vulnerable spot between helmet and shoulder
pads, Hayes hit Bauman with a right uppercut to the neck. In the
ten-minute brawl that ensued, Hayes actually hit one of his own
players. Later, officials hit Hayes with two fifteen-yard penalties
for unsportsmanlike conduct.

The next day, Hayes, who had won 238 games at Ohio State,
was fired.

A shocking event off the field cut short
Lyman Bostock's $2.5 million career.

Billy vs. George-I

On January 3, 1973, a group headed by George M. Steinbrenner
purchased the New York Yankees from CBS Television. Three
years later, Steinbrenner hired fiery manager Billy Martin for the
first time. On July 24, 1978, Steinbrenner and Martin parted ways
for the first time.

Technically, Martin resigned, giving way to Bob Lemon. In a
curious move five days later, Steinbrenner announced that Martin
would be back as manager, in 1980.

BOSTOCK SHOT DOWN

Lyman Bostock was a pure hitter, a free-agent commodity who
had commanded a $2.5 million, five-year contract before the 1978
season. On September 28, 1978, he left the potential tying run on
second base by grounding out, dressed quickly, and stormed out
of the California Angels visiting locker room at Comiskey Park.

Later that evening, Bostock attended a dinner party in Gary,
Indiana, with his uncle and two women. According to police

reports, the estranged husband of one of the women stalked them and unloaded a shotgun into the back seat where Bostock sat. He died three hours later.

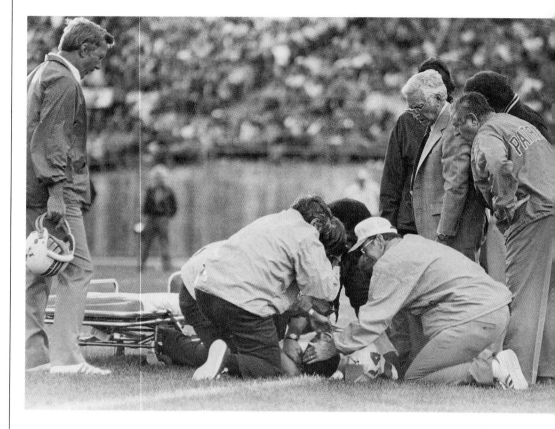

In professional football, the object is to win. This is often achieved by intimidation. In 1978, Oakland Raiders defensive back Jack Tatum crashed into New England Patriots wide receiver Darryl Stingley. It was a meaningless exhibition game and the pass was clearly overthrown, but Stingley was crippled for life.

TATUM LEVELS STINGLEY

Darryl Stingley, the twenty-six-year-old wide receiver for the New England Patriots in 1978, ran the precise steps of his crossing pattern, spotted the ball, and launched himself. He had caught two consecutive passes for forty yards in this August 12, 1978, exhibition game at the home of the Oakland Raiders, but late in the second quarter this one was clearly out of reach. Nevertheless, he stretched for the ball.

Jack Tatum, the safety for the Raiders, crouched in the middle of the field and sprinted as Stingley made his move. They met in midair and Stingley, who instinctively ducked his head before contact, went down. The crowd cheered, but Stingley never got up. Never.

"I could have attempted to intercept," Tatum wrote later in his autobiography, *They Call Me Assassin.* "But because of what owners expect of me when they give me my paycheck, I automatically reacted to the situation by going for an intimidating hit. You hate to see anyone hurt, but I was just doing my job."

After lying motionless for ten minutes, Stingley was removed from the field on a stretcher. Later, doctors determined that Tatum's blow had fractured the fourth and fifth vertebrae in Stingley's neck and damaged his spinal cord. Stingley survived, but he had been rendered a quadriplegic.

Today, Stingley is the Patriots' executive director of player personnel. He works from a wheelchair. Tatum, whose stock dropped quickly after his vicious (but legal) hit on Stingley, is out of football.

HEY, TERRY, CAN YOU SPELL C-A-T?

The Super Bowl has always been the clear-cut hype leader among American sporting events. For a week, more than 2,500 media types on expense accounts mill around a city like Miami, New

"Because of what owners expect of me when they give me my paycheck, I automatically reacted to the situation by going for an intimidating hit. You hate to see anyone hurt, but I was just doing my job."

Over the years, the drama at the Super Bowl has been confined to the week leading up to the game, not the event itself. Super Bowl XIII provided one of history's best one-on-one matchups: Pittsburgh quarterback Terry Bradshaw against Dallas linebacker Thomas "Hollywood" Henderson.

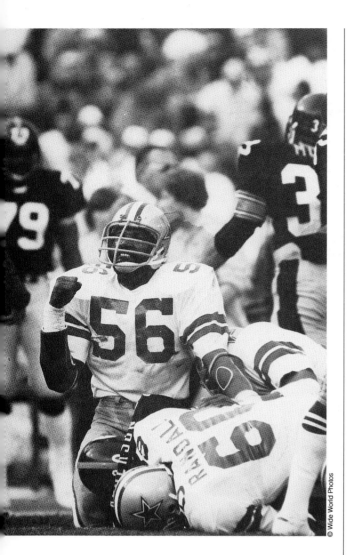

Though Hollywood Henderson openly questioned Terry Bradshaw's spelling ability, Bradshaw spelled W-I-N in Super Bowl XIII.

Orleans, or Los Angeles looking for something, anything, to write about. Non-stories become stories. Good stories become legend.

That was the backdrop when Thomas "Hollywood" Henderson, a linebacker for the Dallas Cowboys, gave the media the kind of colorful copy it craved at Super Bowl XIII in Miami in January 1979. The Cowboys, reigning Super Bowl champions, met the Pittsburgh Steelers, who were looking for their third crown in five years. Steelers quarterback Terry Bradshaw had completed eighteen of thirty-three passes for 305 yards and three touchdowns with no interceptions, in back-to-back Super Bowl victories in 1975 and 1976.

"I'm not extremely brilliant and have never claimed to be," Bradshaw once said. "But I can study a tendency chart on the defense and select the plays that will work in a given situation. This isn't nuclear physics, it's a game....How smart do you have to be?"

Hollywood Henderson begged to differ. Super Bowl XIII, he said, would be won by the smarter team. Dallas quarterback Roger Staubach, he said, was a gentleman and a scholar. Bradshaw on the other hand, couldn't spell "cat" if "you spotted him the 'c' and the 'a.' "

In retrospect, this was probably not the wisest tack. In one of the greatest Super Bowls in history, Bradshaw had a game for the ages. He completed seventeen of thirty passes for 318 yards and four touchdowns. Pittsburgh beat Dallas 35-31 and Bradshaw couldn't resist this tease to reporters: "Go ahead," he said amid the post-game celebration. "Ask Henderson if I was dumb today."

'TOO TALL' TRIES BOXING

Ed "Too Tall" Jones was coming off his best season as a professional football player when the idea first gripped him. He had recorded twelve quarterback sacks for the Dallas Cowboys in 1978, but it was almost too easy. After appearing in Super Bowl XIII he decided he needed a new challenge. He took up boxing.

Jones won all six of his professional fights, though the opponents were little more than journeymen. Jones returned to play

© Wide World Photos

defensive end for the Cowboys in 1980 and resumed one of the brightest careers in franchise history. He was voted to the Pro Bowl three straight years. By 1989 he had knocked down more passes (eighty-two) than any player in memory, proving his best knockdowns had, in fact, come outside of the ring.

KUHN BANS MAYS

Willie Mays, one of baseball's most exciting players, was that rare combination of speed and power. He hit 660 home runs and stole 338 bases in twenty-two seasons. Mays was rarely thrown off-stride on the field, but in 1979 Baseball Commissioner Bowie Kuhn staggered Mays with a cheap shot.

Six years after he made his last appearance for the New York Mets, Mays was approached by an Atlantic City, New Jersey, casino. They wanted him to shake hands with the high rollers and

Call it a mid-career crisis. Ed "Too Tall" Jones left the security of big-time football in 1979 to pursue a boxing career. After six fights, he discovered that he enjoyed decking quarterbacks more than boxing opponents. The pay was better, too.

lend his great name, his cachet, to the enterprise. Mays said "yes," then Kuhn said "no." Fearful that the integrity of the game was at stake, Kuhn banned Mays from having any connection at all with baseball. In 1983, he made a similar ruling concerning former New York Yankees' slugger Mickey Mantle.

In 1985, after Kuhn had given way to Peter Ueberroth, Mays and Mantle were reinstated. After their ludicrous exile, they could again attend games and appear in old-timers' contests.

Knight strikes

Bobby Knight, the volatile coach of the University of Indiana men's basketball team, always seemed to produce disciplined, successful teams. If only he could apply the same discipline to his own wayward temper. In July 1979, he was arrested and charged with aggravated assault on a police officer while coaching the American entry in the Pan-American Games. He was convicted in absentia to six months in prison.

MUNSON CRASHES

He was the conscience of the New York Yankees in the late 1970s, the captain who carried the team to three World Series championships in four seasons. While most of the Yankees enjoyed a day off in August 1979, Munson was practicing landings and takeoffs in his small Cessna jet. He had only held his license, No. 15NY, for a brief time, but true to form, he was working hard to perfect this new craft.

Less than 1,000 feet from the runway at the Akron-Canton airport near his home in Canton, Ohio, Munson lost control of his million-dollar plane and crashed. The force of the crash dislocated Munson's cervical vertebrae and he later died of asphyxiation. His two passengers survived.

Later that season the Yankees retired pinstriped uniform number 15 forever.

© Hy Peskin/FPG International

In a ridiculous ruling, Baseball Commissioner Bowie Kuhn banned former slugger Willie Mays from baseball when he went to work for an Atlantic City, New Jersey, casino in 1979.

Thurman Munson played the game of baseball on the edge; he gave everything he had to the enterprise. The New York Yankees catcher lived his life that way as well. Munson loved to fly. In 1979, the small plane he was flying crashed, effectively ending an era for the Yankees.

Billy vs. George–II

On June 18, 1979, New York Yankees owner George Steinbrenner fired manager Bob Lemon. Billy Martin, who had already managed the team for a three-year stretch, was the replacement. It was the fourth managerial change in the seven seasons Steinbrenner had owned the Yankees, but he was just warming up. Four months and ten days later, Martin was gone for the second time, replaced by the late Dick Howser.

CLASSEN, 29, DIES IN RING

Middleweight fighter Willie Classen was not a top-ranked boxer with a national following. He fought for a living because it was all he knew, and he took pride in his work.

On November 23, 1979, he met the talented Wilford Scypion at Madison Square Garden's Felt Forum in New York City. Clearly, Classen was in over his head. For Scypion, it was business as usual and he dispatched Classen with an unremarkable tenth-round knockout.

Five days later, however, the bout made headlines. Classen had suffered brain damage during the fight and had died at Bellevue Hospital at the age of twenty-nine. Classen's death, one of four ring tragedies in a span of several months, opened a new debate on the dubious merits of the sweet science.

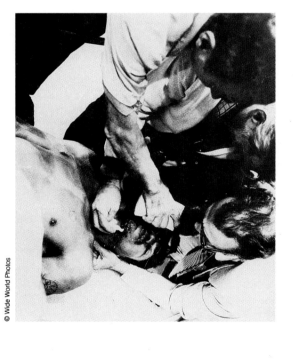

© Wide World Photos

For years, the debate has raged: Should boxing be banned? In 1979, the ring death of middleweight Willie Classen gave boxing's critics some new ammunition.

Wham! Bam!

He called himself "Chocolate Thunder," and it was an apt name for the cartoon that was Darryl Dawkins. He was close to seven feet tall and more than 250 pounds of sculpted muscle with a penchant for rhyming descriptions of his basketball exploits. Nothing he came up with compared to the majesty of his achievement in 1979. In a span of twenty-two days, Dawkins destroyed not one, but two glass backboards in his quest for the perfect slam-dunk.

The opening ceremonies of the 1980 Summer Olympics had the full complement of Eastern-Bloc countries, but the United States was conspicuously absent.

CARTER BOYCOTTS MOSCOW

Before Glasnost and the falling of the wall in Berlin, the cold war between the United States and the USSR regrettably spilled over into the athletic arena. On January 4, 1980, President Jimmy Carter announced, "Regardless of what other nations might do, I would not favor the sending of an American Olympic team to Moscow while Soviet invasion troops are in Afghanistan."

And so, the United States did not send its athletes to the Summer Olympics in Moscow. They were joined by West Germany, Canada, and Japan. In the opening ceremony, sixteen of the eighty-one competing nations refused to carry flags. In 1984, the USSR returned the favor, opting to keep its athletes home while the world competed at the Summer Olympics in Los Angeles.

RUIZ RUNS UNDER COVER

Rosie Ruiz, wearing number W-50 across her orange jersey, flashed across the finish line of the Boston Marathon. Her arms were outstretched, her smile golden. Looking back on the spring of 1980, Ruiz just seemed a trifle too fresh.

Humiliated by the taunting of Sugar Ray Leonard, Roberto Duran turned his back on Leonard and the boxing world in 1980.

Soon afterward, Massachusetts Governor Edward King placed a laurel wreath over her dark curls and presented her with a gold medal signifying her victory in the women's competition. It wasn't until later that Ruiz was revealed as an imposter. She had pulled off one of the great undercover operations in sports history. Ruiz joined the twenty-six-mile race in its late stages and crossed the line well ahead of the lead women's pack.

In truth, Canada's Jackie Gareau was the winner and Ruiz was disqualified. Eventually, Gareau received all the spoils of victory that were due her, but as United States competitor Joan Benoit lamented, "Jackie was denied forever the thrill of her greatest moment."

DURAN QUITS: 'NO MAS!'

The second meeting of boxers Roberto Duran and Sugar Ray Leonard was sharply anticipated around the world. In their first welterweight fight in Montreal, Duran had triumphed with a gritty

fifteen-round unanimous decision. Now, five months later, the scene moved to the New Orleans Superdome.

Obviously, Leonard had gone to school in that first bout. He came into the November 25, 1980, fight enormously wiser. When Duran tried to intimidate him by clutching and grabbing, Leonard countered with similarly rough tactics. By the fifth and sixth rounds, Leonard's laser foot speed left Duran swinging at the air. He grew increasingly frustrated.

During the seventh round, Leonard began to mock Duran. He stuck his tongue out, offered his chin and took it away, and displayed a fair rendition of the Ali Shuffle. With less than twenty seconds left in the eighth round, after Leonard had scored at will, Duran turned his back and walked toward his corner. "No mas," he said, waving his glove in disgust. "No mas."

Later, Duran would blame stomach cramps for his ignominious defeat, though it was clear the once-proud fighter, known in his native Panama as "Los Manos de Piedras" (Hands of Stone), had been humiliated. Though Duran fought for nearly another decade, he never carried quite the same hubris into the ring again.

BASEBALL STRIKES OUT

For more than a century, baseball had thrived in the marketplace of America and avoided the painful labor disputes that dogged other businesses. That is, until 1981. Sure, the first thirteen days of the 1972 season had been canceled, and in 1980 eight exhibition games fell by the wayside. But for the first time in the history of the great game, the strike of 1981 interrupted a season in progress. On June 22, with fifty-odd games in the books, the players walked off the job.

When the owners and the players finally found common ground, the season was more than half over. The solution? A split season. The standings before the strike were frozen and a second half was played, primarily in August and September. The Philadelphia Phillies and Los Angeles Dodgers, leaders in the first half, played the Montreal Expos and Houston Astros in a best-of-five playoff series for the right to meet for the National League pennant. In the American League, the New York Yankees and Oakland A's played the second-half champs, the Milwaukee Brewers and Kansas City Royals. Ultimately, the Dodgers beat the Yankees four games to two in a World Series that punctuated baseball's most fractured season.

'MACHINE GUN' MOLLY GIVES BEST SHOT

Beauty, of course, is in the eye of the beholder, but perhaps the best shot in basketball history occurred far off the court.

That's right. It was a wonderful eighteen-by-twenty-four-inch, black-and-white poster that featured "Machine Gun" Molly Bolin. It was shot in April of 1981, and the star of the Iowa Cornets was featured wearing a dark bathing suit and was surrounded by a basketball and her sneakers. The figure she cut was well-rounded, to say the least.

"Hey," she reasoned, "it's all about putting people in the seats, isn't it?" Alas, Bolin and the Women's Basketball League she represented faded from the sporting landscape quite quickly. The memory of that remarkable poster, however, lingers with anyone lucky enough to have seen it.

KING AND HER COURT

Rumors concerning women's tennis and the gay lifestyle had circulated for years, but in May 1981, the innuendos became headline news.

Marilyn Barnett, a former hairstylist who had served as Billie Jean King's secretary, claimed that she and the tennis star had shared romance over several years in the 1970s. Barnett brought suit against King seeking lifetime support and threatened to reveal intimate details of their alleged affair. Initially, King denied the charge. Then, to her credit, she decided to meet the threat head on and took the matter public. With her husband Larry at her side, surrounded by cameras and microphones, King admitted she had made a mistake.

Seven months later in California, Judge Julius Title agreed, but ruled that Barnett had no grounds in her palimony suit. King had won but she had also spent more than a quarter-million dollars in legal expenses. She found little joy in victory. "The fact is," King said, "I could never win. I'll never be the same. I'll never recover from the damage I suffered, the emotional damage to me and Larry, and my folks. But...you have to go on."

RAIDERS LEAVE OAKLAND

The posturing had begun several years earlier, when the Oakland Raiders joined the Los Angeles Coliseum Commission's antitrust suit against the National Football League. The Raiders and owner, Al Davis, unhappy that the league would not approve a move from Oakland to Los Angeles, joined the parade that believed the league had violated antitrust laws.

On May 7, 1982, a jury ruled against the NFL in the Raiders' antitrust suit. That gave Davis clearance to move his team to Los Angeles. In their first game in their new home on August 29, the Los Angeles Raiders defeated the Green Bay Packers 24-3 at the Los Angeles Coliseum.

NFL PLAYERS WALK OFF JOB

For several years, the players of the National Football League had seethed as owners rang up record profits while their salary curve remained relatively flat. In 1982, Ed Garvey and Gene Upshaw did something about it. Garvey, the executive director of the NFL Players Association, and Upshaw, the union president, organized the first regular-season strike in the league's sixty-three-year history.

The walkout began at midnight, on September 20, minutes after a Monday night game between the New York Giants and

Green Bay Packers. For fifty-seven days, the players sat out as the owners and the players tried to reach a collective bargaining agreement. On November 17, the players won a minimum salary schedule based on experience, improved training camp, and post-season pay, as well as increased medical insurance and retirement benefits.

Seven of the sixteen regular-season games were lost and the league radically altered its playoff format to accommodate the shortened season. Sixteen of the NFL's twenty-eight teams made the playoffs, the so-called Super Bowl tournament. Ultimately, the Washington Redskins beat the Miami Dolphins 27-17 in Super Bowl XVII at the Rose Bowl in Pasadena.

Above: **It was high-fives all around for the Washington Redskins as they beat the Miami Dolphins in Super Bowl XVII. The long, rancorous strike that preceded that triumph, however, strained the relationship between National Football League players and management and it has yet to heal.**
Right: **Renaldo Nehemiah could run faster and jump higher than nearly all of his National Football League peers. The only problem? He wasn't much of a pass receiver.**

A new hurdle for Nehemiah

Renaldo Nehemiah had already conquered world-class track and now it was time for something completely different. The six-foot-one, 177-pound hurdler owned thirteen indoor and outdoor world records, including the blistering 12.93-second mark in the 110-meter high hurdles he set in the summer of 1981. After several years at the top of his game, Nehemiah's motivation suffered.

The San Francisco 49ers, always looking for an edge, liked what they saw of the would-be wide receiver on the practice field. Nehemiah could run, jump, and, more often than not, he could catch the football. Running pass routes in the NFL's congested secondaries was another thing, though. In three years with the 49ers, Nehemiah caught a respectable forty-three passes for 754 yards and two touchdowns. After the 1984 season, he walked away from football forever.

MANCINI LOWERS THE BOOM ON KIM

Duk Koo Kim of South Korea was an honorable boxer who had been taught to give the most to his craft. In November 1982, he gave the ultimate, his life, in a bout with Ray "Boom Boom" Mancini.

Mancini, the popular lightweight champion from Youngstown, Ohio, was one of boxing's leading lights in the early 1980s. He was personable, refreshingly honest, and an exciting, aggressive fighter. After knocking out Art Frias in the first round to claim the World Boxing Association title, he met Kim, the WBA's leading contender. Most experts figured Kim, twenty-three, would go the way of Frias in a swift fight. They were wrong.

At Caesar's Palace in Las Vegas, Kim pushed Mancini all the way to the fourteenth round of the scheduled fifteen-round fight. Two thunderous right hands by Mancini dropped Kim to the canvas and, with nineteen seconds left in the round, he was counted out by the referee. Kim never fully regained consciousness. He was taken to a nearby hospital, where doctors worked for nearly three hours to relieve a subdural hematoma. Four days later, Kim was removed from the respirator that was keeping him alive.

The tragedy reopened the debate over boxing's place in sports, but officials ruled that it couldn't have been helped. Apparently, doctors said, a small vessel in Kim's brain had been ruptured by a Mancini punch late in the bout. Mancini, for his part, was never quite the same. He lost his title to Livingstone Bramble in 1984 and by 1985 he was out of boxing completely.

SCHLICHTER GAMBLES WITH FUTURE

Like it or not, drugs, sex, and rock and roll have always been part of the landscape in professional sports. They have been accepted by administrators, to some extent, as a necessary evil. Gambling, and its implications of something less than fair play, has never fallen into that category. Just ask Paul Hornung or Pete Rose.

On the surface, Art Schlichter had it all. He was a large, gifted quarterback who had led Ohio State to the Rose Bowl title. He was drafted by the Indianapolis Colts in the first round of the National Football League draft and eventually signed a big multi-

The Colts' horseshoe was never lucky for quarterback Art Schlichter; after four difficult seasons in the National Football League, his history of gambling finally caught up with him.

year contract in 1982. It wasn't until a year later that the Colts discovered their strong-armed quarterback was too good to be true.

Reports surfaced that Schlichter had blown more than one million dollars in his senior year at Ohio State and his rookie year in the NFL. Schlichter, it was reported, was cooperating with authorities investigating a Baltimore-area gambling ring. This was his response when the gamblers allegedly threatened to blackmail him by making his gambling affliction public.

Schlichter was suspended in May 1983 and underwent counseling before the Colts reinstated him in 1984. He played in only ten more games before Indianapolis released him for good, claiming his arm was too weak to pass muster in the NFL. A year later, the Buffalo Bills came to the same conclusion. Schlichter never really recovered from that rejection. In 1987 he was arrested for gambling hundreds of thousands of dollars.

Morganna titillates baseball

In June 1983, the general public finally discovered Morganna, baseball's kissing bandit. The Kentucky-based stripper of staggering dimensions (60-24-39) appeared in a fully orchestrated *Playboy Magazine* layout that left little to the imagination.

Morganna got her start in the national spotlight on the baseball field. On the dare of a girlfriend, Morganna jumped out of the stands one day in Cincinnati in 1970, and bussed Reds star Pete Rose. As time passed, Morganna refined her act of trespassing to an art form. Over the years she chased down Nolan Ryan, Mike Schmidt, and Steve Garvey. She was arrested once in Houston, but her lawyer argued that the sheer size of her chest spilled her from her front-row seat and onto the field. The charges were dropped.

THE (IN)FAMOUS PINE TAR INCIDENT

George Brett, the Kansas City Royals' third baseman, trotted slowly around the bases and crossed home plate on July 24, 1983. His teammates engulfed him. Brett had apparently just burned

He will go down as one of the best hitters baseball has ever seen, but George Brett will always be remembered for a sticky wicket and as the "Pine Tar Incident" of 1983.

"It didn't feel like it was a victory," said New York third base- man Graig Nettles. "It was just an ugly win with an asterisk."

© Don Smith/Allsport

reliever Goose Gossage with a game-winning, two-run homer to beat the hated New York Yankees with two out in the ninth inning. Billy Martin, the Yankees manager, smiled and strolled to the plate.

He pointed to Brett's bat and informed the umpires that it didn't conform to major-league rules. The brown, sticky pine tar that many hitters used to improve their grip extended far beyond the eighteen-inch (46 cm) limit from the bat handle. Martin had known of Brett's penchant for pine tar for some time and stored this seemingly useless piece of information away for a moment like this. And though the sticky stuff clearly did not affect the flight of the ball, umpires had no choice but to agree with Martin. The Yankees were declared 4-3 winners.

The spirit of the rule, however, was quite another thing. "It didn't feel like it was a victory," said New York third baseman Graig Nettles. "It was just an ugly win with an asterisk."

Four days later, American League President Lee MacPhail essentially agreed with him. He reversed the umpires' decision and ordered the game to resume on August 18. The Royals' 5-4 win held up this time and Brett's place in history was secure. Forget that he was a perennial .300 hitter. "They're going to remember the pine tar," he says. "Kind of funny, isn't it?"

As Royals' second baseman Frank White said, "I don't know if it was part of history. But this way, we all sort of get into the Hall of Fame at the same time."

Liberty, **skippered by Dennis Conner, won three of the first four America's Cup finals races in 1983, but lost the last three and surrendered the silver trophy for the first time in 132 years.**

AMERICA'S CUP RUNNETH OVER

Twelve-meter racing is sport at its glorious pinnacle. Gorgeously colorful spinnakers, swollen in the wind, cut a dashing figure against the sea and sky. It was thus in the summer of 1983, when the United States and Australia waged a compelling water war for the America's Cup.

© Wide World Photos

Liberty, the American boat, led the best-of-seven match three races to one when a curious thing happened: *Australia II*, skippered by John Bertrand, won three consecutive races. The Aussies surged past the Americans on the fifth leg of the final race and crossed the finish line, impossibly, first. That's when the real war began, only this one was played out not in the water, but within the domain of the courts.

The Australians, financed by Perth businessman Alan Bond, had won with a radical and controversial keel designed by Ben Lexcen. Large pieces of lead in each of its two fins gave the boat a remarkable stability in heavy air and, at the same time, maneuverability in light air. For the first time in 132 years, the America's Cup left the sanctity of the trophy case at the New York Yacht Club.

The Americans had challenged the keel in court, but the Aussies had prevailed. In the bitterness that followed, the Cup lost much of its luster. After winning it back, the Americans, within the rules, insisted that the race be contested in hulking catamarans. That option was later struck down by a judge, an action that left yachting enthusiasts hoping that future America's Cup races would be decided on the water, where they belonged.

SEALES A SIGHT FOR SORE EYES

All that glittered was Sugar Ray Seales in 1972, when he won the gold medal in the 134-pound boxing class at the Summer Olympics in Munich, West Germany. Eleven years later, at the age of thirty, Seales could hardly see.

His woes began in 1980, when he suffered a detached retina in a fight with Jamie Thomas. Nevertheless, he was at it again four months later, fighting in Indiana. He boxed with damaged eyes in six different states because, incredibly, he passed the mandatory physicals. As his sight faded, Seales rationalized that this was merely a part of his savage profession.

"I was waiting for the real people to stop me," he said later. "Each time I'd say 'one more,' I was waiting for the real people to say, 'Your one more was last time.'"

"Each time I'd say 'one more,' I was waiting for the real people to say, 'Your one more was last time.'"

© Wide World Photos

The eyes, in this sad case, did not have it. Sugar Ray Seales raised his arms in triumph in this 1980 victory, but nineteen years in the ring would ultimately leave him virtually blind.

Ultimately, it was Seales who blew the whistle on himself. After nineteen years of boxing, as both an amateur and a professional, Seales finally left the ring for good. According to doctors, basically he was blind in his left eye and had only 10-percent vision in his right.

"I can't read," Seales explained. "I can't drive. Most I can do right now is walk with this cane."

Billy vs. George – III

The last time the New York Yankees had seen Billy Martin was October 1979, when owner George Steinbrenner fired him and made Dick Howser his sixth manager in seven years. On January 11, 1983, Martin returned for his third tour of duty, following Howser, Gene Michael, Bob Lemon, and Clyde King. Less than a year later, on December 16, 1983, Martin was fired again.

IRSAY TAKES COLTS FANS FOR A RIDE

It was still 'round midnight on March 28, 1984, when the moving vans slipped away from Baltimore with all the footballs, helmets, and uniforms. At the same time, a million memories that included a victory in Super Bowl V and a roster of Hall of Fame names like Johnny Unitas, Lenny Moore, Raymond Berry, and Al Parker were wrested from the city that had so embraced them over the years.

Certainly, professional sports franchises had moved their scene of operations before, but never in such startlingly covert fashion. Baltimore owner Robert Irsay, unhappy with local fan support and eyeing a more attractive leasing situation at the Hoosier Dome, took his team to Indianapolis, Indiana.

Quite naturally, the citizens of Baltimore were as outraged as Indianapolis was overjoyed. After the 1987 season, fans in St. Louis could relate to the misery in Baltimore. Their football team, the Cardinals, packed up and moved to Phoenix.

BUDD DECKS MARY DECKER

Finally, after years of disappointment in important international track events, Mary Decker was about to enjoy her finest moment. It was the final of the 1984 Summer Olympic Games 3,000-meter race and a partisan crowd at Los Angeles Memorial Coliseum cheered her on.

The pre-race hype had centered on Decker and Britain's Zola Budd and, sure enough, they literally tangled as the race wore on.

© Vandystadt/Allsport

Budd, running in her trademark bare feet, caught Decker's ankle with her foot and Decker went down in a heap. She rolled into the infield and sobbed as the race continued. It was Decker's last real chance at an Olympic gold medal. Zola continued but finished out of the running.

Later, Decker had the grace to say, "I know what Zola did was intentional. You can tell."

The women's 3,000-meter race in the 1984 Summer Olympics goes on, but Mary Decker is left behind. Her collision with Zola Budd, leading on the inside, reduced her to tears and touched an entire nation.

Marques capsizes

On June 11, 1984, the 117-foot British ship *Marques*, one of forty-two entries in the Bermuda-Nova Scotia leg of the Tall Ships races, sank in stormy seas. Nineteen of the twenty-eight-person crew died.

Fixx dies on the run

Jim Fixx, the celebrated running and fitness author, died while jogging in 1984. He was fifty-two.

© Trevor Jones/Allsport

The crowd loved Anne White's daring all-white body suit, but Wimbledon officials sent White and her ground-breaking outfit to the showers.

257 strokes wins golf title

Under the most intense competitive pressure of his thirty-one years, Angelo Spagnolo came through in the clutch. He fashioned a remarkable (what other word is there?) 257 to win the Worst Avid Golfer Tournament, sponsored by *Golf Digest*. The Pittsburgh golfer brutalized the Tournament Players Club course at Ponte Vedra, Florida, in June 1985 with some frighteningly ugly hacks at the ball. His crowning glory was a sixty-six on the picturesque seventeenth hole. After hitting countless balls in the water to all sides of the virtual island green, Spagnolo gently tapped his ball a dozen feet at a time up the narrow passage that connects tee and green.

Anne all-White affair

The Wimbledon tennis club outside of London, England, has a tradition all its own: tennis on grass, strawberries and cream, all-white apparel. In June 1985, Anne White followed the letter of the dress code but pushed the spirit of the tournament into the twenty-first century. She took to the court wearing a clingy, all-white body suit and displayed a rather lithe, uh, backhand. The suit was quickly banned by Wimbledon, but White had already made a bold fashion statement.

Buoniconti paralyzed

His father Nick had been a heralded linebacker for the Miami Dolphins, but Marc Buoniconti had been carving out a niche of his own when tragedy struck on October 26, 1985. A linebacker for The Citadel, Buoniconti was just doing his job when he put his head down and crashed into East Tennessee State running back Herman Jacobs. Jacobs got up; Buoniconti did not.

His spinal cord had been severed and he was paralyzed from the neck down. Buoniconti could not breathe without the aid of a respirator. Father and son became the focal point of a fundraising drive that generated millions of dollars in an effort to discover a cure for spinal paralysis.

Billy vs. George–IV

On April 28, 1985, ridiculously early in the season, New York Yankees owner George Steinbrenner fired Hall of Fame catcher Yogi Berra as his manager and named Billy Martin as his successor. It was Martin's fourth tour of duty at the helm of the Yankees. It lasted one day short of six months. On October 27, Martin was dismissed for the fourth time and replaced by Lou Piniella.

LINDBERGH DIES IN CRASH

Pelle Lindbergh, one of the best and brightest in the National Hockey League, was the league's reigning goalie in 1985. He had produced a 40-17-7 record and won the Vezina Trophy the season before, an award based on fewest goals allowed. He had shown signs of repeating the feat. In November, however, the Swedish goalie missed a turn, lost control of his apple-red Porsche, and smashed into a concrete wall. He died within hours of extensive brain and spinal cord injuries.

Witnesses reported that Lindbergh had been celebrating a Philadelphia Flyers victory, in which he did not play, by drinking heavily at two bars. Later, authorities reported that the level of alcohol in Lindbergh's blood stream was between .17 and .24, an extraordinarily high number. Police reports suggested that Lindbergh had been traveling in excess of eighty miles an hour and hadn't hit his brakes until he was almost on top of the wall.

COCAINE KILLS BIAS, ROGERS

As drugs infiltrated American society in the late 1960s and early 1970s, there were few immediate signs that they had reached the world of athletics. Professional and top-notch collegiate athletes, after all, were basically a conservative lot and they had their careers

© Al Messerschmidt

Above: Don Rogers was an intimidating defensive back for the Cleveland Browns, but he couldn't handle cocaine. Opposite page: Len Bias could do it all on the basketball floor, but cocaine cost him his life.

to think of. In 1963, football star "Big Daddy" Lipscomb had died of a heroin overdose, and in 1970 Pittsburgh Pirate pitcher Doc Ellis had thrown a no-hitter on LSD, but these were thought to be isolated cases. In the early 1980s, the major professional and college sports leagues seemed to be winning the war. Then in 1986 came the deaths of Len Bias and Don Rogers only four days apart.

Bias was, by all accounts, an All-American in every sense of the phrase. He was a star forward for the University of Maryland basketball team and his 2,149 points were a school record. When the Boston Celtics made him their first-round draft choice, the National Basketball Association officials predicted a long run of success. He was young, articulate, and gifted. On June 23, 1986, he was pronounced dead after ingesting cocaine. It was believed that the drug caused convulsions and spasms that created blood clots, which blocked an artery. The heart that the Celtics prized so highly stopped beating.

Rogers had already made a mark in the professional ranks as a cornerback for the Cleveland Browns. When he died on June 27 after a cocaine overdose, a nerve was exposed.

"We're close to a genocide of our young people," said Harry Edwards, a nationally prominent sociologist at the University of California at Berkeley. "Bias and Rogers are the first wave of the drug-culture generation. These are kids who grew up inside drugs."

The message was straightforward: Athletes are people too, and susceptible to the same pleasures and pains that afflict their fans. Alcohol, the drug of choice for many athletes in the spotlight over the years, gave way to cocaine. Their salaries and lifestyle made it easily attainable. Between 1984 and 1988, the number of cocaine-related deaths more than tripled, from 628 to 2,234. Between 1985 and 1988, the estimated number of Americans who used cocaine at least once a week increased 29 percent, to more than 1.1 million people. According to a Senate Judiciary report issued in 1990, the figure is now almost twice that.

"We are now fighting two drug wars, not one," said William Bennett, director of the Office of National Drug Control Policy at

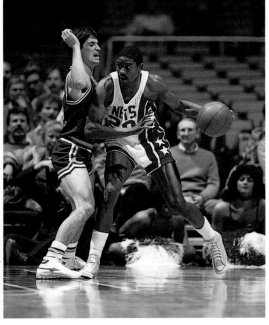

Michael Ray Richardson of the New Jersey Nets (*above*) and the New York Giants' Lawrence Taylor (*right*) both worked their magic at the Meadowlands in East Rutherford, New Jersey. Both of them succumbed to the evils of cocaine. Taylor overcame his addiction to complete a Hall of Fame career; Richardson was banished from basketball before his time.

the time. "The first and easiest is against casual use of drugs, and we are winning it. The other, much more difficult, war is against addiction to cocaine. And on this second front, increasingly located in our cities, we are losing badly. Undeniably, the fact remains that here in the United States, in every state, in our cities, in our suburbs, in our rural communities, drugs are potent, drugs are cheap, and drugs are available to almost anyone who wants them."

The laundry list of athletes with cocaine problems is exhausting and cuts across all disciplines. A partial roster: baseball players Keith Hernandez, Dwight Gooden, and Willie Wilson; basketball player Michael Ray Richardson; and Lawrence Taylor, perhaps the finest linebacker in the history of the National Football League.

Like Bias, Taylor thought he was indestructible. Certainly, at six-foot-three, 240 pounds, Taylor was one of the fastest men for his size in the game. Asked what he could do that other linebackers couldn't do in 1986, the New York Giant responded, "Drink." It was that penchant for alcohol that led to cocaine. The problem first surfaced in 1985, but after outpatient treatment in Houston that basically consisted of a lot of golf, Taylor felt he was cured. Three years later, Taylor was undergoing treatment again after a second positive test for cocaine.

"I thought I had it under control because I was doing it the way I wanted to do it," he said. "I wouldn't let the Giants or my wife help me. Early in training camp I only drank Perrier but as things progressed I had a couple of beers, which turned into a couple of mixed drinks. One night I made a bad decision. I didn't mean for it to happen, and now I'll pay the price for it."

"I am an addict. I'm not worried about what's going to happen in thirty days: I'm worried about what's going to happen the rest of my life. Getting straight is all I'm worried about."

The NFL, NBA, and major league baseball have all implemented stringent drug policies that involve testing. The NFL calls for a thirty-day suspension after two positive tests. In 1988 alone, the NFL suspended twenty-four players for violating the policy. After Taylor's fall from grace he battled the addiction and has subsequently stayed clean. A third strike means banishment for at least one season. Cincinnati Bengal Stanley Wilson, Tony Collins of the New England Patriots, and Dexter Manley have all suffered that fate. Manley, the Washington Redskins' all-time leader in quarterback sacks and the team's defensive leader, was banned for life late in the 1989 season. Manley was reinstated in 1990, cut by Washington, and was signed by Phoenix.

As Taylor said in 1988, "Football players are just like everybody else. Yeah, we might get paid more, but drugs is everywhere. People don't want to hear it, but it's in sports. You could test sports writers and truck drivers and find it there, too."

KEMP CHALLENGES GEORGIA ATHLETICS

Ah, the wonder of the big-time college athletic system. Football and basketball players between the ages of eighteen and twenty-two generate millions of dollars for their schools' athletic departments and, in theory, receive nothing in return except a decent education. And they do this with a smile on their faces. Well, not quite. When television money raised the stakes significantly in the 1970s, amateur athletics changed forever. Recruiting became a cutthroat business. In some places, money and favors changed

© Lee Wardle/Sports File, Inc.

Defensive end Dexter Manley resurfaced in Phoenix after the Washington Redskins cut him loose in 1990.

hands. Usually, the hypocrisy of the system remains under the surface. Fortunately, every few years a courageous person like Jan Kemp comes along to remind us that college athletics has some serious flaws, that education isn't always the first priority.

Kemp, the coordinator of the English section of the University of Georgia's Developmental Studies Program, was fired after she charged that the school gave athletes preferential treatment with respect to academics. Not convinced that the two events were unrelated, she sued. The six-week trial that unfolded in the winter of 1986 revealed a program that seemed more interested in keeping its athletes eligible for competition than creating the environment for a real education. The trial made national headlines and begged the troublesome question: Should college athletes be paid for their performances?

Kemp won her case. She was awarded $2.58 million and another $1.5 million in punitive damages. And although college athletics is still fraught with cheating and hypocrisy, the American public's perception of the "purely amateur" system is slowly changing. Kemp, among others, hopes the college rules and regulations will one day reflect that changing sentiment.

THE USFL COMES UP A $1 WINNER

There was a time, during the 1920s to be precise, when professional football was something on the level of professional wrestling. Over the years, however, the game has gained momentum and today the National Football League is big business. Naturally, everyone wants a piece of the considerable action. One of the reasons Pete Rozelle retired as league commissioner in 1989 was the many antitrust suits he was forced to endure.

The usual complaint: The league violates antitrust laws by monopolistic behavior among its twenty-eight clubs. The Oakland Raiders jumped on the bandwagon in 1980, claiming that the NFL wronged them by declining to approve a move to Los Angeles. As it turned out, the Raiders and owner Al Davis won that case. The United States Football League, one of several pretenders to the

NFL throne in recent years, did not.

For a second-tier league, the USFL was extremely well financed. Donald Trump and John Bassett were among the owners and they helped secure a television contract with ABC in 1984 that gave the league a degree of instant credibility. In time, though, the fans stopped going to games. In 1986, the USFL did what many NFL officials had been predicting for years. They sued for $1.7 billion. The eleven-week trial made national headlines as the fledgling league sought to prove that NFL administrators had conspired behind closed doors to drive the USFL out of business.

On July 29, a jury in U.S. District Court in New York awarded the USFL a single dollar but rejected the claim that the NFL tried to pressure the networks into dumping the USFL. Twenty months later, the Second Circuit Court of Appeals upheld the verdict in a unanimous 3-0 decision. Judge Ralph K. Winter summed it up nicely, saying the USFL sought "through court decree the success it failed to gain among football fans."

Some of Willie Gault's best moves came on the dance floor.

Gault proves a good sport

As a world-class sprinter, Willie Gault was aesthetic in his own way as he churned around the track with his high-leg kick. In his second career as a wide receiver for the Chicago Bears, Gault was fierce enough to deal with all the fire-breathing tacklers that came his way. In October 1986, Gault climbed into a third arena. He performed for charity in a ballet with the Chicago City Company. And, according to the critics, he wasn't bad. "It took a lot of guts for me to do that," Gault said. "But I wanted to show that ballet wasn't a sissy sport." The next night, Gault caught seven passes for 174 yards against the Cincinnati Bengals.

CAMPANIS GOES DOWN SWINGING

The man from ABC's Nightline was asking about the dearth of black managers in baseball, and indeed, in management overall. Al Campanis, a respected baseball man from the Los Angeles

"It took a lot of guts for me to do that," Gault said. "But I wanted to show that ballet wasn't a sissy sport."

73

Dodgers, opened his mouth and swallowed both his feet during the 1987 television interview. Blacks, he said, "may not have some of the necessities" for management positions.

What followed was a firestorm. Campanis was only speaking his mind and expressing a sentiment that many unenlightened people in baseball (and out) shared; however, he was not in a back room playing cards and drinking beer with his buddies. This opinion was magnified under the bright lights of national television. Campanis, as well as the baseball establishment, was charged with racial discrimination, considering that many of the on-field performers are minorities. When the backlash grew intolerable, the Dodgers were forced to fire him. And though several black managers subsequently have been named, the management landscape in baseball remains largely white.

BASEBALL'S CHEATING RASH: JUICED BALLS, CORKED BATS

For a game that is at times both lyrical and sublime, baseball has had its share of ugly incidents. The Chicago Black Sox scandal, the Curt Flood challenge, and the Pete Rose affair have all become part of the history. One thing people forget, though, is that baseball is in many ways a game based on deceit. Why do you think they invented spitballs, anyway?

For many observers, 1987 was the season that baseball's devious colors were revealed. Billy Hatcher of the Houston Astros opened the debate, so to speak. Actually, his bat opened up, revealing an illegal cork center. Hitters will tell you that by replacing heavy oak with the lightness of cork, the bat head is allowed to move more quickly through the strike zone. Result: a heavier, deeper hit. Hatcher's indiscretion, underlined by the historic number of home runs flying out of ballparks, led to a lot of jumping at dugout shadows. New York Mets slugger Howard Johnson was often accused of corking but was never found guilty of the illegal practice.

Pitchers were not exempt from what Yankees hurler Tommy John called "a witch hunt." Philadelphia Phillies pitcher Kevin Gross was caught with a tack in his glove, which might have explained his sharp control. He was suspended. Hitters claimed that Mike Scott of the Houston Astros scuffed his baseballs in an attempt to get quirkier movement out of his fastball. He was searched several times, but nothing incriminating was found. But when umpires visited Minnesota Twins knuckleball artist Joe Niekro at the mound during a game against California, they asked to see the contents of his pockets. An emery board was seized. Though Niekro claimed he used it between innings to keep his nails trimmed for better control of his knuckler, the skeptics smiled. Here was evidence, after a fashion, that baseball was still driven by the art of deception.

© Rick Stewart/Allsport

In a case of gross misconduct, Philadelphia Phillies pitcher Kevin Gross was caught with a thumbtack in his glove in 1987.

When the lights came back on at Boston Garden in 1988, the Edmonton Oilers were on their way to winning the Stanley Cup.

Lights out in Boston

On May 24, the Boston Bruins and the Edmonton Oilers were battling it out in the fourth game of the 1988 Stanley Cup Final. Thirty-seven minutes into the game, the score was tied at three-all when the lights went out. Really. The creaking Boston Garden, a fifty-nine-year-old building, had been showing signs of age for years, but this was too much. A 4,000-volt switch overloaded and the arena was blacked out. Eventually, the game resumed and, ultimately, the Oilers won the Stanley Cup. The Boston Garden, however, was condemned. In several years, the Bruins and Boston Celtics will be playing in a new arena.

ROSE BUMPS PALLONE

Pete Rose, always the hard-charging baseball player, finally lost control in May 1988. In the middle of a fiery argument with umpire Dave Pallone, Rose seemed to poke Pallone in the face. Pallone pushed back and promptly tossed Rose out of the game. A few days later, Rose was tossed out of baseball for thirty days by Baseball Commissioner Peter Ueberroth, the longest such suspension in forty-one years.

Billy vs. George – V

When we last saw Billy Martin, he was cooling off after his fourth dismissal by New York Yankees owner George Steinbrenner in 1985. Two years later, on October 19, 1987, his successor Lou Piniella was kicked upstairs and Martin was brought back for another tour as manager. His fifth and final reign lasted less than a season. Martin was fired on June 23, 1988, and replaced, naturally, by Piniella.

STEROIDS USE COSTS JOHNSON OLYMPIC GOLD

The world had long awaited this confrontation and now, at the 1988 Summer Olympic Games in Seoul, South Korea, Canadian Ben Johnson and Carl Lewis of the United States eyed each other warily in the starting blocks before the 100-meter final. More than 70,000 spectators looked on at Olympic Stadium, but it was *no lo contendre*. Johnson burst from the blocks, opened a startling lead in the first ten meters, and won with astonishing ease. As he coasted past the finish line, Johnson glared at Lewis, who was running three

Ben Johnson arrogantly eyed runner-up Carl Lewis at the finish line of the 1988 Summer Olympics' 100-meter final, but his performance was just another example of better technology through chemistry. Johnson was stripped of the gold medal when traces of steroids were discovered in his system.

lanes away, and extended his right index finger aloft, reconfirming his status as the world's fastest human. Johnson was clocked in 9.79, breaking his own world record by four-hundredths of a second. Lewis' 9.92, an American record, was a relatively distant second.

Johnson, whose huge thighs and shoulders seemed more appropriate for a shotputter, was in fact too good to be true. Johnson, who had passed a drug test a year earlier when he set the world record in Rome, tested positive for stanozolol, an anabolic steroid, after his race at Seoul. He was stripped of his gold medal and the new record in a turn of events that rocked the athletic world. Five months later, in a Toronto hearing room, track coach Charlie Francis revealed that Johnson began using anabolic steroids in 1981 and continued regularly until the Summer Games. Francis, known in Canadian track circles as "Charlie the Chemist," testified before Canada's Commission of Inquiry into the Use of Drugs and Banned Practices Intended to Increase Athletic Performance. The panel, formed in the wake of Johnson's ignominious departure from Seoul, discovered that the scope of illegal drug use to enhance track performances was mind-numbing.

According to Francis, steroids were worth about a meter in a 100-meter race. At the world class level of track, that 1-percent

After being banned from competition, Johnson returned to the track in 1991. Without steroids, he was merely a mediocre world-class runner.

© Tony Duffy/Allsport

improvement was everything. "He could decide to set up his starting blocks at the same line as all the other competitors," Francis said, "or set them up a meter behind them all. And, obviously, that would not be acceptable for a top-level athlete." Francis testified that thirteen of the athletes he had coached used steroids and that he had heard rumors while competing at the 1972 Olympics in Munich, West Germany, that 80 percent of the best athletes were using steroids. And though, as Francis testified, anabolic steroids have been on the world-class scene for some time, Johnson focused global attention on the subject for the first time.

Just what are steroids? A synthetic derivative of the male hormone testosterone, steroids promote increases in protein synthesis in skeletal muscle cells. Steroids were developed more than fifty years ago to help prevent the breakdown of tissue that occurs in some debilitating diseases. The Germans administered steroids to some of their army soldiers in World War II because it made them notably more aggressive. By 1950 bodybuilders had become aware of their muscle-enhancing qualities. Athletes in sports where more muscle means more power and, therefore, greater success, began to experiment with steroids.

Over time, they discovered that by using steroids, lifting weights religiously, and eating a diet heavy in protein and carbohydrates, twenty pounds of muscle could be created in less than three months. Users also reported an increase in aggression and a frame of mind that allowed them to work harder and longer in the weight room.

Players in the National Football League, particularly those who played in the trenches along the offensive and defensive lines where raw strength overpowers finesse, began using steroids regularly in the 1970s. Former Raiders star Lyle Alzado has stated publicly that steroids use is rampant in the NFL; he attributes the rare form of brain cancer he suffers from to his own long-term steroid use. In May 1989, Atlanta Falcons guard Bill Fralic testified at a United States Judiciary Committee hearing that 75 percent of the NFL's linemen used steroids. "High school players think they need steroids to win a college scholarship," he said. "College

"High school players think they need steroids to win a college scholarship, college players do steroids so they can improve their chances at playing in the pros and getting a lucrative contract. NFL players use steroids to keep their jobs."

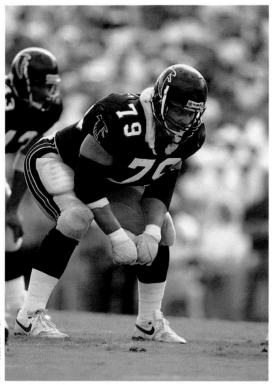

© Al Messerschmidt

Atlanta Falcons offensive lineman Bill Fralic was one of the few football players to admit that steroids were a part of life in the National Football League.

players do steroids so they can improve their chances at playing in the pros and getting a lucrative contract. NFL players use steroids to keep their jobs."

In the 1990s, steroids will have inexorably trickled down to the high school level. According to a 1987 survey that appeared in the Journal of American Medicine, 6.6 percent of all eleventh-grade males polled said they had used steroids. In a 1988 survey for the national Youth Sports Coaches Association, Dr. Michael Gray discovered that 2 percent of the nation's ten-to-fourteen-year-old athletes had already used steroids. That doesn't seem like a big number," Gray says, "but consider that there are ten million athletes in that age group. That works out to 200,000 kids under high school age who are users. Based on the statistics, it's going to go up for some time. That's a frightening situation."

The United States Food and Drug Administration estimates that sales of black-market steroids eclipse the $100 million mark annually. National experts say 80 percent of the steroids used illegally are distributed in gyms, particularly those that feature free weights and are frequented by serious bodybuilders.

"The scary thing about steroids is that they've been around for years...and nobody knows anything about them," says Herb Strickland, a senior agent for Connecticut's Department of Consumer Protection's drug control division. "They've been in the locker room all that time, and now the door has been broken down. Ben Johnson made steroids big news."

ROSE GAMBLES WITH A FUTURE IN HALL OF FAME

He was the most prolific hitter in baseball history, the model of determination and grit for a generation. In the spring of 1989, however, all the records (4,256 base hits, 3,562 games played, 15,890 plate appearances) were forever tainted when it was alleged that Pete Rose had bet on baseball games in the mid-1980s. One of those teams he bet on, it was alleged, was the one he managed,

© J. Zehrl/FPG International

Pete Rose managed his Cincinnati Reds from the base paths. Did he make bets from the dugout, too?

the Cincinnati Reds. Suddenly, his 1992 election into the Hall of Fame at Cooperstown, New York, that had seemed so absolutely certain was very much in doubt.

Former bookmaker Ron Peters told John Dowd, baseball's chief investigator in the case, that he took bets from Rose through a series of intermediaries at his restaurant, Jonathan's Cafe in Franklin, Ohio. According to Peters, Rose sometimes placed the bets by telephone himself and wagered in excess of $1 million over a three-year period. When other witnesses corroborated much of Peters' testimony, Baseball Commissioner A. Bartlett Giamatti concluded that Rose had broken baseball rule 21 (d), which prohibited gambling, and had no choice but to suspend him from baseball for life. Giamatti recommended that Rose seek help for his gambling affliction.

The same defiant manner Rose exhibited between the foul lines sometimes manifested itself off the field in greediness and an inclination to choose some unsavory friends. Rose needed cash to fuel his habit and, apparently, he used his good name to maximum effect. Collectors of baseball memorabilia suggest that there are

© William Hart/Allsport

The Hit, the 4,192nd of Pete Rose's career, was dramatically cheapened when word of his gambling activity surfaced in 1989.

more than a few bats in circulation with which Rose claimed to get his record-breaking 4,192nd hit. The same is true for uniform shirts, spikes, and jerseys. Rose, a favorite with autograph collectors, could earn in excess of $20,000 for a single autograph session at baseball card shows.

Rose also had a lucrative endorsement contract with the Mizuno sporting goods company of Japan. In 1981, government officials say he failed to declare more than $46,000 in cash on his return from Japan. Five years later Rose repaid half that amount in a penalty. In January 1989, Rose was allegedly part of a winning Pik Six ticket at Turfway Park in Florence, Kentucky, that paid $265,669. Rose, apparently, did not declare the winnings and was investigated by the federal government for possible tax evasion. Rose, according to friends, is also a high roller at the Las Vegas casinos and bet often on the National Football League and college football games in addition to baseball.

But Rose lost heavily on football. "Baseball," according to Peters, "was what he knew, and he felt like he had to get some of his money back that he lost. And he did. He was good at betting baseball."

Rose was proud and defiant to the end. At spring training in 1989, he refused to admit he had bet on baseball. He denied that he had a problem. Even when a grim Giamatti announced he was suspending Rose for life, the old ballplayer shook his head. The nickname "Charlie Hustle," given to him as a rookie in 1963, took on a new and insidious meaning.

WORLD-CLASS SNEAKERS OFFER LICENSE TO KILL

Johnny Bates was just another sixteen-year-old kid with a dream and a slick pair of hightop basketball sneakers. One day in April 1989, seventeen-year-old Demetrick Walker asked Johnny to hand over his Air Jordans. Johnny refused. Walker shot him dead, over a $100 pair of sneakers. Walker is serving a life sentence in jail and prosecutor Mark Vinson says, "It's bad when we create an image of luxury about athletic gear that forces people to kill over it."

The incident was by no means isolated. In Detroit, Los Angeles, Philadelphia, and New York City, kids are killing kids over stylish athletic wear. Why? With more than $7 billion in annual sales, the athletic shoe and sportswear industries have worked hard to cultivate the cachet that comes with high-priced luxury items. One of the big markets for this line of merchandise is America's inner cities, where money and labels constitute instant status. Often that money is generated by drugs or gangs, or both.

Michael Chasen, a Chicago police sergeant who works in the city's violent crimes division, says the districts his group oversees (less than 20 percent of Chicago) respond to nearly fifty incidents involving upscale athletic jackets and about a dozen concerning athletic shoes a month. He told *Sports Illustrated*'s Rick Telander, "When you really think about the crime itself, taking someone's clothes off their body, you can't get much more basic."

Chasen was right. A life for a pair of sneakers? The athletic shoe industry alone spent more than $200 million promoting its products last year and deserves at least some of the credit for warping society's values to the extent that these incidents have become commonplace.

Spike Lee, the filmmaker who appears with Chicago Bulls superstar Michael Jordan in Nike commercials for Air Jordans, was attacked by several national columnists. "The problem," Lee wrote in an editorial in *The National*, a defunct sports daily, "is not the shoes. Let's try to effectively deal with the conditions that make a kid put so much importance on a pair of sneakers, a jacket, and gold. These kids feel they have no options, no opportunities."

GATHERS COURTS DISASTER

Outwardly, Hank Gathers was a six-foot-seven, 210-pound piece of work, a combination of controlled power and fury that Michelangelo might have crafted from Italian marble. The Loyola Marymount (California) College senior was one of the nation's finest basketball players and he was poised for his finest moment in the 1990 National Collegiate Athletic Association tournament when two forces conspired to kill him on March 4. First, there was his abnormal heartbeat. Second, his insatiable appetite for competition.

There had been trouble before. On December 9, he fainted on the court during a game against the University of California-Santa Barbara. The irregular heartbeat was discovered and Gathers was given an antiarrhythmic drug to control the problem. After sitting out two games, Gathers was back in the lineup. "As far as we knew, it was safe for him to play," said Dr. Mason Weiss of the Daniel Freeman Marina Hospital in Marina del Rey. "He was taking his medication."

Perhaps. According to those familiar with Gathers, he complained that the drug prescribed by Dr. Vernon Hattori left him moody and sluggish. Moreover, it affected his ability to play basketball. Eventually, Hattori relented and Gathers' dosage was

"This is the hardest thing I've experienced," said red-eyed coach Paul Westhead. "To be so close to a player and see him fall and for it to be over..."

reduced. Gathers, who had hoped to be one of the first of a handful of players picked in the upcoming National Basketball Association draft, improved his scoring and rebounding averages to twenty-nine and eleven. Still, those numbers weren't quite up to his phenomenal 1988-89 season, when he became only the second Division I player in history to lead the country in scoring and rebounds (32.7, 13.7) in the same season.

Loyola Marymount's reputation for running and pressing made the school one of the favorites for a berth in the NCAA tournament, but first there was the small matter of the West Coast Conference tournament. Gathers was anything but sluggish. Less than seven minutes into the first half of a semifinal game with Portland, Gathers showed the NBA scouts what he was made of,

In some ways, Hank Gathers was a victim of himself. His dazzling athletic skills might have blinded him to his own mortality.

taking a pass in midair and slamming it down in one spectacular motion. Then, as he turned to head back on defense, Gathers stumbled and fell. Two hours later he was dead. "This is the hardest thing I've experienced," said red-eyed coach Paul Westhead. "To be so close to a player and see him fall and for it to be over…"

Heart failure was the coroner's official verdict, but there was an undercurrent of feeling that Gathers shouldn't have been allowed to play, even if it meant dashing his dreams of playing professional basketball. The entire story may never be known.

After the playoff game and the tournament were canceled, WCC officials selected Loyola Marymount, the regular-season champion, to represent the conference in the NCAA tournament. After a long discussion, the team decided to play and dedicate its performance to Gathers. Loyola Marymount, seeded eleventh in the West Region, beat higher-seeded teams without Gathers in three consecutive victories to reach the quarterfinals against impossible odds. The University of Nevada at Las Vegas, the eventual champion, beat Loyola Marymount when talent finally overcame emotion and the memory of Hank Gathers.

GRETZKY SOLD DOWN THE RIVER

Just when you think you're safe, when you've put in a few good years at the home office, along comes that gruesome transfer notice. In August 1988, it happened to the greatest hockey player in history.

Less than a month after he wed actress Janet Jones, the Edmonton Oilers essentially sold Wayne Gretzky to the Los Angeles Kings of the National Hockey League. Edmonton owner Peter Pocklington, suffering from a cash-flow problem, sent "The Great One" to La-La Land for a hot $15 million, plus three first-round draft choices.

The trade was a bombshell and Canada's newspapers reacted with typical nationalistic zeal. It was front-page news for days. As it turned out, the trade helped both teams. Edmonton went on

Quick, what's wrong with this picture? Somehow, the sight of Wayne Gretzky playing in anything but an Edmonton Oilers uniform is unsettling.

to win another Stanley Cup and the Kings gained credibility in Los Angeles, where the Lakers used to be the only real major-league team in town.

OKLAHOMA FOOTBALL FALLS UNDER SCRUTINY

For as long as anyone can remember, college football players have lived by a code all their own. They are young and strong and live without responsibilities off the field. On January 26, 1989, according to the Federal Bureau of Investigation, University of Oklahoma quarterback Charles Thompson sold seventeen grams of cocaine for $1,400 to an undercover agent. He had been the Sooners' leading rusher the previous season but he wasn't going to run very far behind bars.

Over the next few months, the lawlessness on the Norman, Oklahoma, campus came into focus. Allegations of sexual misconduct, trigger-happy players, and stories of cash and cars to recruits dogged head coach Barry Switzer. This after the National Collegiate Athletic Association had placed the Oklahoma team on probation for three years. Switzer eventually left.

The problems were by no means particular to Oklahoma. *Sports Illustrated* reported that at least two dozen football players at the University of Colorado had been arrested in a three-year period, dating from February 1986. Players were charged with everything from trespassing to drunken driving to rape. Somehow, the Colorado program rose to national prominence in 1989. Maybe there was a connection.

'MARGOGATE' PUTS PRESSURE ON BOGGS

Even today, Wade Boggs of the Boston Red Sox is the leading active hitter in major league baseball. His lifetime batting average still hovers around the ethereal .350 plateau, a figure surpassed by a mere handful of men in history. Boggs has always been a player blessed with uncommon powers of concentration, but in the spring and summer of 1989 he was forced to draw on all of his abilities.

That was when the story of Margo Adams broke in the nation's sporting press. News of a tell-all story in *Penthouse* magazine found the Red Sox at spring training in Florida. Adams was Boggs' traveling companion for four seasons of road trips. The trouble was, Boggs was married with children. Adams' charges came to light even before the article appeared when she sued Boggs, claiming she was due compensation for expenses and lost wages on those trips. The newspapers had a field day. Trade rumors swirled.

Typically, Boggs was unruffled by all the hoopla. After all, he had won the 1986 American League batting title after his mother died that June in an automobile accident. "My head hits the pillow," he told reporters at spring training, "and I'm out. I'm not going to let this person destroy my world. You just have to be a strong person."

In a quiet moment, he was less blustery. "I've learned a lot in the last eight months," he said. "The best thing that ever happened to me was getting caught. It's made my marriage so much better. You realize, I could have thrown this whole thing away for nothing. But Debbie understood. Having the strength of my wife with me after having done something like that to her for four years made me realize, man, love is the strongest thing in the world."

Boggs somehow managed to hit .330 in 1989, but for the first time since 1984 he hit under .357 and did not win the American League batting title. A year after the storm broke in Florida, Boggs was again a relatively anonymous figure in the batting cage. "It's like day and night," he said. "My life is back to normal."

Safe to say, Wade Boggs was not a hit in his own home over the summer of 1989.

Earthquake rocks 1989 World Series

The Bay Area had already suffered major tremors leading up to the 1989 World Series. And why not? The Oakland A's had won the American League pennant and the San Francisco Giants, neighbors from across the Bay, had taken the National League flag. And then, on October 17, the gentle buzz of pregame activity for game

© Otto Greule Jr./Allsport

three at Candlestick Park was interrupted by a savage earthquake. The battle of the Bay became a struggle for survival.

Lives and homes were lost. A portion of the Bay Bridge became dislodged. Candlestick Park itself suffered minor damage. The game was, correctly, postponed by Baseball Commissioner Francis T. Vincent Jr. "It is becoming very clear to all of us in major league baseball that our concerns, despite this rather large gathering, our issue is really a modest one," he said, "in light of the great tragedy that hit this area." Ten days later, after the rubble had been cleared in San Francisco's Marina District and the city was slowly returning to normal, the Series resumed. In the years ahead, most people won't remember that the A's laid waste to the Giants. They'll remember the day the earth moved at Candlestick.

McENROE ACED 'DOWN UNDER'

At his best, John McEnroe was a stylish, left-handed artist on the tennis court. He was the best in the game in the early 1980s. At his worst, McEnroe was a sad court jester, consumed by the demons within.

But even in his young, wild days, McEnroe was never tossed from a tournament. And yet, in the 1990 Australian Open,

McEnroe became the first player in twenty-two years of Open tennis to be ejected from a Grand Slam tournament for misbehaving. Here is how it happened:

By all accounts, McEnroe had mellowed considerably since taking time off to start a family with actress Tatum O'Neal. Still, he did not seem aware of the new rules that governed his sport when he took to the court for a fourth-round match at the National Tennis Center in Melbourne. Previously, players cited four times in a match for unsportsmanlike conduct were to be expelled. The 1990 rule clearly stated that players would receive only three strikes before they were ejected from the game.

As McEnroe rolled out to a 6-1, 4-6, 7-5, 2-4 lead over Mikael Pernfors, he was his usual blustery self. Umpire Gerry Armstrong took note. McEnroe was warned for approaching a lineswoman in the third set after a call he contested. He smashed his own racket in the fourth set and received a second warning. McEnroe, furious, asked for an audience with the umpire chief, who predictably supported Armstrong. As he shuffled back onto the court, McEnroe disparaged the chief's mother and received the third, and fatal, warning. Game, set, and match to Pernfors.

McEnroe sulked. "After you've played for three hours, I think it was unnecessary to disqualify me for a four-letter word," he said. "I think there should be better discretion."

John McEnroe argued his point, but umpire Gerry Armstrong made his more emphatically: McEnroe was bounced from the 1990 Australian Open in historic fashion.

© Pascal Rondeau/Allsport

PISTONS AND 76ERS COME OUT SWINGING

It was, the participants agreed, one of the wildest fights in the history of the National Basketball Association. Certainly, it was the most expensive.

The fisticuffs late in the 1989-1990 season involved two of the most physical teams in professional basketball, the Detroit Pistons and the Philadelphia 76ers. With less than four minutes left in a game that was rapidly eluding the Pistons, Detroit point guard Isiah Thomas threw a punch at former teammate Rick Mahorn. It barely touched Mahorn's shoulder, but Thomas was ejected.

With fifteen seconds left, Mahorn emphatically slam-dunked the ball to give Philadelphia a 107-95 lead. Detroit's Dennis Rodman, who hadn't liked Mahorn's insult-to-injury intent, fouled him. Detroit center Bill Laimbeer emphasized Rodman's point by pushing the ball into Mahorn's face. That was when Philadelphia's Charles Barkley, not a big fan of Laimbeer's, drilled him with several punches. The benches cleared, but instead of the usual milling around, there were blows exchanged for about ten minutes.

The NBA executives spent the next few days reviewing tapes of the scrap and their ultimate penalties were staggering. Laimbeer and Barkley were each fined $20,000, while Detroit's Scott Hastings was fined $10,000. Five other players drew minimal penalties, but the teams were fined $50,000 for failing to control their players. The grand total was $162,500, a record for fighting in a professional game of any kind.

SPORTS SALARIES REACH THE OZONE

Even in the mid-1970s, respectable baseball players were earning modest five-figure salaries. But as the 1980s blurred into the 1990s, America's professional athletes were rapidly crashing the exclusive territory that once belonged to corporate raiders and movie stars. Now, it seems, even middle-of-the-road singles hitters can make $1 million a season. Journeymen basketball players take home $2 million.

In the span of a few months in the summer of 1990, two Bay Area athletes became the highest-paid athletes in the history of their respective sports. Jose Canseco, the slugger for the Oakland A's, signed a four-year contract that was worth more than $16 million. In 1990, he made $4.7 million, or roughly $536 an hour, twenty-four hours a day. San Francisco 49ers quarterback Joe Montana worked out a four-year, $13 million deal that paid him $4.0 million in 1990. The scary part? Their employers could afford it, based on revenues. That would explain rising ticket prices in professional sports.

Is this man worth $14 million? The Los Angeles Rams thought so.

The price of winning in sports has increased so sharply that Oakland A's slugger Jose Canseco and New York Mets pitcher Dwight Gooden earn more in a day than many people earn in a year.

It was 1990 that marked a new era in salaries for professional athletes. Baseball pitchers Dwight Gooden, Roger Clemens, and Orel Hershiser are all $3 million men. Why, Darnell Coles of the Seattle Mariners received $510,000 in 1989 to hit .252. In football, the quarterbacks cleaned up. Before Montana signed his lucrative deal, Randall Cunningham agreed to an eight-year, $19.55 million deal with the Philadelphia Eagles, the Los Angeles Rams' Jim Everett inked an estimated six-year, $14 million pact, and the Cleveland Browns' Bernie Kosar took home a seven-year, $16 million deal.

Basketball, because of the relatively low number of players on each team, has always paid its players best. New York Knicks center Patrick Ewing made $4 million in 1989, which was the high end of the National Basketball Association scale. But, seriously, was Jon Koncak really worth a whopping $2.2 million? Even though his career scoring average was just 6.2 points at the time, the Atlanta Hawks thought so. Nevertheless, there are even bargains in the NBA. While Koncak was pulling down the big dollars,

Bargain basement: Joe Dumars was the Detroit Pistons' most valuable player in the 1989 league championship. He was a steal, at $890,000 annually.

© Rich Kane/Sportschrome, Inc.

Detroit Pistons guard Joe Dumars was winning the most valuable player award in the league championship series. His price? A low, low $890,000.

And then there is boxing. In 1989, Sugar Ray Leonard brought in nearly $30 million. And that was for two fights. Heavyweight Mike Tyson was next, at $14 million. He fought all of six rounds, which works out to $848,484 per minute. And they say professional athletes are overpaid.

32-DAY LOCKOUT WIPES OUT SPRING TRAINING

As the price for tickets and television rights spirals upward, professional athletics becomes more and more a business and less an entertaining sport. In the spring of 1990, the owners of major league baseball clubs and their players faced off in a battle for turf and a bigger piece of the billion-dollar pie. The result was a thirty-two-day lockout that basically ruined the spring training schedules in Florida and Arizona.

Not only did the fans miss out on Grapefruit and Cactus Circuit games, but the local economies built around spring training suffered badly. So did the condition of the players, who worked out on their own. The dispute was resolved on March 19, perilously close to the scheduled opening day.

"Neither side is particularly happy," said Chicago White Sox owner Jerry Reinsdorf. "But this kind of thing was inevitable."

Reinsdorf was one of five owners on the Player Relations Committee that hammered out a four-year collective bargaining deal with the Players Association on March 19. The players seemed to collect on most of their demands.

The key issue was the time at which players would become eligible for salary arbitration. It was agreed that some players between two and three years of major-league service (the 17 percent with the most service) would be eligible. Previously, only players with three years of service or more had been eligible. The reason the players pursued the issue with such vigor: The 162 players that filed for salary arbitration in 1989 received raises that averaged more than 100 percent, or $430,000. However, the new formula for eligibility expanded the potential arbitration pool by only a dozen or so players.

The new contract also raised the minimum salary from $68,000 to $100,000, improved the owners' annual pension contribution from $39 million to $55 million, and called for a roster expansion from twenty-four to twenty-five players, beginning in 1991.

After a mere two weeks of exhibition games, the 1990 regular season opened a week late. The baseball establishment took a lot of abuse in the national press, but the widespread injuries that were predicted due to a lack of training never came to pass. The real injury came at the ticket offices, where fans began paying for the new price of doing major-league business.

'The Boz' gets released

Brian Bosworth, the man who called himself "The Boz," was a college phenomenon. He was a devastating force as a linebacker at the University of Oklahoma, leading the team in tackles in each of his three years for a total of 395. Bosworth also won the Dick Butkus Award in 1985 and 1986 for being the nation's best linebacker. Even after he was sidelined from a post-season bowl game after anabolic steroids were discovered in his urine sample, Bosworth was the first pick in the 1987 supplemental draft. The Seattle Seahawks, in a sweep of generosity that baffled many National Football League administrators, gave him an $11-million contract that ran through 1996.

After three middling seasons, Bosworth was out of the NFL and the Seahawks were left holding the bags. The money bags.

Of the forty-eight games Seattle played during his tenure from 1987-89, Bosworth started and played at inside linebacker in only

Brian Bosworth never lived up to his self-generated hype. As a linebacker for the University of Oklahoma and, later, the Seattle Seahawks, he was serviceable but ordinary. He was still on Seattle's payroll when he launched his movie career in 1991.

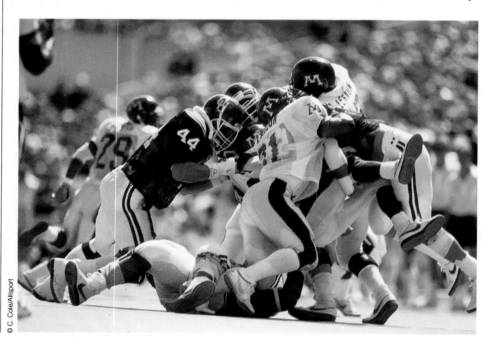

twenty-four. In his first two seasons, the six-foot-two, 236-pound Bosworth finished second and third in tackles but was slowed by a series of injuries. Ultimately, a chronic shoulder condition was his undoing. He played in only two games in the 1989 season and the Seahawks waived him before the 1990 season. According to the original contract, Seattle was forced to pay the retired player a guaranteed $600,000 in 1990 and $700,000 in 1991.

LYONS DROPS HIS DRAWERS

The first thing you need to know about Steve Lyons is that his Chicago White Sox teammates call him "Psycho." What is more, he likes the nickname. The next item for discussion is the act that will keep Lyons' name alive for decades.

Q: Which ballplayer actually pulled his pants down during a game?

A: Steve "Psycho" Lyons.

It's true. On July 16, 1990, at Detroit's Tiger Stadium, Lyons bunted and charged down the line to first base. He leaned forward and dove. In a cloud of dust he was ruled safe by the umpire. As the Tigers argued the call, Lyons, in a typical moment of self-absorption, pulled down his uniform pants and absentmindedly brushed the dirt that had collected on his midsection. The players on the field stopped in their tracks. The fans went crazy; some women waved dollar bills in his direction.

Fortunately, Lyons was wearing underwear at the time. He says he may try to follow Hall of Fame pitcher Jim Palmer and model underwear in his second career. On the other hand, "After seeing those women wave dollar bills at me," Lyons says, "I think I could be a pretty good stripper."

Roseanne Barr hits low note

As a singer, Roseanne Barr is a great comedienne. That was the unanimous review after she sang, well, attempted to sing *The Star-Spangled Banner* on July 26, 1990, at San Diego's Jack

Murphy Stadium.

Barr was asked to perform by Tom Werner, the San Diego Padres' chief of operations and the producer of Barr's television show, *Roseanne*. What came out was a screeching mess that left the fans in the stands speechless. And then the boos began. Barr, who later said she was parodying the way baseball players scratch themselves, scratched at her crotch three times and spit before she left the field.

The response from the San Diego community, where there is a large military population, was uniformly harsh. Outrage also poured in from across the nation. President George Bush called it "disgraceful."

Barr responded, "I'm sorry that I didn't sing so good, but I'd like to hear him [Bush] sing it."

A UNIFORM DISGRACE

Little League, as many people know, is a game kids play for fun, but is often taken too seriously by adults. In the summer of 1990, nearly a year after the Trumbull (Connecticut) Nationals won the Little League World Series at Williamsport, Pennsylvania, that theme came home again.

Matt Sewell, twelve, had been one of fourteen players selected for the Trumbull All-Star team and he had played well in right field. He hit .500 and fielded his position with grace. And then, in the middle of the tournament, he broke his wrist while delivering newspapers. According to Little League rules, Sewell was replaced by an alternate and essentially banned from contact with the team. He wasn't allowed to sit in the dugout during games. He wasn't permitted to travel on the team bus or stay in the team quarters. When his teammates received green and gold uniforms at Williamsport bearing the legend "EAST," Sewell could only be jealous.

After Trumbull defeated Taiwan in the championship final, Little League officials broke a precedent. Since it was the fiftieth anniversary of Little League, the boys were allowed to keep their

The report stopped short of recommending paying students to represent an institution, or denying admission to athletes unqualified to do college-level work. It did not grapple with the issue of revenue-sharing that might further reduce the incentive to break the rules. Until the difficult issues are debated, college athletics will continue to operate without any clear master.

DYKSTRA, DAULTON IN CRASH

Lenny Dykstra took to calling himself "Nails" when he played for the New York Mets, but toughness wasn't enough to avoid injury in the wee hours of May 6, 1991. Dykstra, the Philadelphia Phillies' outfielder, and catcher Darren Daulton were driving home from the bachelor party of teammate John Kruk when Dykstra lost control of his red 1991 Mercedes and struck two trees in Radnor, Pennsylvania.

The damage was complete: Dykstra sustained multiple fractures, including a broken collarbone and a broken cheekbone, a punctured lung, and a bruised heart. Daulton also suffered a bruised heart and a broken eye socket. According to police, Dykstra was intoxicated, well over the legal alcohol limit. Daulton was released from Bryn Mawr Hospital after a few days, but Dykstra was in for over a week and was expected to miss more than two months of the season.

© Wide World Photos

On May 6, 1991, Phillies outfielder Len Dykstra lost control of his luxury automobile. Less than two months later, he was taking batting practice with his teammates again.

FURTHER READING

Asinof, Eliot. *Eight Men Out*. New York: Holt, 1963.

Garber, Angus G. *The Baseball Companion*. New York: Mallard Press, 1990.

Garber, Angus G. *Baseball Legends*. New York: Gallery Books, 1989.

Garber, Angus G. *The Basketball Companion*. New York: Mallard Press, 1992.

Garber, Angus G. *Boxing Legends*. New York: Gallery Books, 1988.

Garber, Angus G. *Champions!*. New York: Mallard Press, 1990.

Garber, Angus G. *Grand Slam*. New York: Gallery Books, 1989.

Gutman, Bill. *The Pictorial History of College Basketball*. New York: Gallery Books, 1989.

Keteyian, Armen. *Big Red Confidential: Inside Nebraska Football*. New York: Contemporary Books, 1989.

Keteyian, Armen. *Catfish*. New York: McGraw Hill, 1989.

Keteyian, Armen. *Raw Recruits*. New York: Pocket Books, 1990.

McCormick, Andrew. *World Cup Soccer*. New York: Mallard Press, 1991.

O'Brien, Rich. *The Boxing Companion*. New York: Mallard Press, 1991.

Sintletary, Mike and Armen Keteyian. *Calling the Shots*. New York: Contemporary Books, 1986.

Telander, Rick. *The Hundred Yard Line*. New York: Simon and Schuster, 1989.

Telander, Rick. *Joe Namath and the Other Guys*. New York: Holt, 1976.

INDEX